Ask the Elk Guides

Ask the Elk Guides

by

J. Y. Jones

SAFARI PRESS INC.

The trademark Safari Press ® is registered with the U.S. Patent and Trademark Office and in other countries.

Jones, J. Y.

First edition

Safari Press Inc.

2005, Long Beach, California

ISBN 1-57157-324-0

Library of Congress Catalog Card Number: 2004094420

10 9 8 7 6 5 4 3 2 1

Printed in the USA

Readers wishing to receive the Safari Press catalog, featuring many fine books on big-game hunting, wingshooting, and sporting firearms, should write to Safari Press Inc., P.O. Box 3095, Long Beach, CA 90803, USA. Tel: (714) 894-9080 or visit our Web site at www.safaripress.com.

This book is primarily intended to promote better understanding between elk guides and elk hunters, and I believe it moves the reader in the right direction. It is to these guides and the hunters who follow them that I dedicate this book, with the sincere hope that good will, better hunting relationships, and ever-increasing ethical hunting behavior will be derived from the efforts embodied in these pages.

I would also like to dedicate this book to those organizations that have been in the forefront of preserving the tradition of elk hunting in North America: the Rocky Mountain Elk Foundation for its unending work in elk conservation; the National Rifle Association for its tireless defense of our right to bear arms; Safari Club International for its aggressive defense of our right to hunt at the local, state, national, and international levels; and the North American Hunting Club for its Wildlife Forever program that benefits conservation of all species.

Lastly, and most importantly, I dedicate this book to my Lord and Savior Jesus Christ, the Creator of the cosmos, who created both elk hunters and elk guides, as well as magnificent elk and the mountains and meadows they inhabit. To Him be the glory!

Table of Contents

Foreword

My friend J. Y. Jones has hit a home run with this book. He's covered all the bases when it comes to hiring an outfitter, and he leaves nothing unanswered. J. Y., a consummate elk hunter, is, undoubtedly, one of the savviest hunters ever to have left boot prints in elk country, and he has left no stone unturned to produce this splendid work.

As one who has hunted elk in every western elk state and all over western Canada, much of the time with outfitters, I wish I could have read this book early on when I still thought that every outfitter was an honest soul who would offer me a fair hunt. I quickly found out that some of those guys wore black hats, and

Wilderness pack-in camp.

some wore white. Unfortunately, realization often came when I was out hunting, which, consequently, was too late to do anything about it. By that time, the hunt would be a disaster, and my memories of it later, a nightmare.

This is not to say that every hunt must result in a guaranteed elk. If that's what you want, go shoot one on a game farm. If, however, you want a fair-chase hunt where you have a reasonable chance of achieving your trophy, read this book carefully and take J. Y.'s advice. It would have been sufficient for J. Y., who is a veteran hunter, to have offered his personal recommendations when searching for an outfitter, but he goes the extra mile and solicits the guys out there who make their living in the elk woods. These are guys like my neighbor Ron Dube, who is one of the finest wilderness elk outfitters I know, and my pal Jack Atcheson Jr., who gets my vote as the toughest hunter/outfitter on the planet. Then there's Al (Big Al) Morris, who has got to be the Pied Piper of elkdom, for when he calls, they come runnin'. And I can't forget John Caid, who no doubt hunts the biggest elk in North America . . . and on and on.

Of course it would be nice if you could hunt with one of the outfitters spotlighted in this book, but that would be impossible. These few guides simply can't handle all the readers. The other option is to carefully read their sage words and apply their logic when you do your homework. Planning is what it's all about. The more time you spend on the phone, the better.

Some surprises in life are pleasant, but unhappy surprises on an elk hunt aren't, and they can be avoided. Do yourself a big favor and follow the advice given here by J. Y. and the excellent outfitters he's selected to share their secrets. They're all within these pages, and I'm mighty proud to have been able to sneak a peek at this book before it was published and add my two cents' worth.

Jim Zumbo
Hunting Editor
Outdoor Life magazine

Jim Zumbo, who has been hunting elk for almost forty years, lives among elk in his northwestern Wyoming mountain home. A prolific writer, he has just completed his seventh elk-hunting book and has written some seven hundred articles on elk hunting.

Introduction and Acknowledgments

I can take credit for neither the idea of this book nor the majority of its content. It is the brainchild of Ludo Wurfbain, owner of Safari Press. He and I shared a wolf hunt in Alberta at one time, and during idle minutes we discussed book ideas. He offered the chance to do this book to a number of his authors, but I was the only one who applied. It was a contest with only one contestant—the easiest kind to win.

The questions are mostly mine, accumulated over years of talking to guides and hunters during hunting excursions and at other times. In order to refine and focus the questions more sharply, I have checked similar books written in other fields, and that was an exercise that greatly improved my original ideas. I have tried to cover questions most hunters would like to put to their guides, but because of pride in their own hunting ability, simple hesitancy, time constraints, the guide's busy lifestyle, or other factors, they seldom get the chance to do so—at least not in thorough fashion. By reading this book, hunters can draw on the knowledge of a dozen top elk guides without leaving the comfort of home. There is a treasure of information documented here that may be unique in literature about hunting in general, and about elk hunting in particular.

One might ask what my qualifications are to interrogate this outstanding group of knowledgeable elk guides. No individual has the expertise even approaching that of all these guides combined, so there is doubtless no single person who could call himself "qualified" by experience or accumulated elk wisdom to delve into their minds. I can only cite my own hunting history and some previous writing experience. I know of no one who has spent more time than I have following a North American big game guide (though there are probably some people out there who have). My guided North American big game hunts now number sixty-five.

I have been on ten elk hunts, ranging from rugged wilderness affairs to comfortable private ranches (including more of the former). Additionally, and by God's matchless grace, I have accomplished what may be one of the most rare achievements in North American hunting, taking what could legitimately be called a Grand Slam of North American Elk. I have now killed all four North American subspecies of elk (using the same .30-06 rifle—See *One Man, One Rifle, One Land*, and recent articles on my taking of the Manitoba subspecies after that book was published.* The Manitoba elk subspecies was not available to non-Canadians when I completed the hunting and writing involved in *One Man, One Rifle, One Land*.)

Selecting the guides was the hardest part of putting this book together. All of the guides chosen hunt only free-ranging wild elk. Some of them I knew already, but the rest I had to contact to solicit their participation. I owe a debt of gratitude to each guide for his enthusiastic cooperation. I am also indebted to many people in my quest to find the very best guides, a mission that I believe has succeeded well. Jack Atcheson, Jr., of Jack Atcheson and Sons, Inc., was the single most helpful individual. He gave me the names of more than a dozen top guides, several of whom appear in the book. Bob Kern of The Hunting Consortium was likewise helpful, supplying several names. My Canadian taxidermist friend and onetime guide, Harvey Daniels, supplied one name. Not surprisingly, a couple of the featured guides supplied their own names, when word got around that such a book was in the making. Ludo Wurfbain himself supplied a name as well.

I have made a determined effort to cover all the different types of Western elk hunting, and to include as many states and provinces as possible. Thus a hunter can choose the sections that best apply to his upcoming hunt, and read what he needs to know about that particular area and that particular guiding situation. The information is authoritative because the material is presented as exact quotations from the guides themselves (with some minor editing).

---

*See *Safari* magazine March-April 2004 and *Big Game Adventures* magazine Summer 2004.

There are likely quite a few guides out there who can legitimately claim to be equal to the dozen featured here, but there will be precious few who would clearly surpass them in their specific area and type of hunting. Probably there are quite a few more who would have made fine contributors to this book, and in fact I contacted, or tried to contact, more than thirty guides before settling on these. Every guide who agreed to participate, who took the time to submit to an interview, and who sent me the appropriate pictures and biographical information has been included. I extend to each one of them my deepest appreciation.

Throughout the book are a number of common abbreviations that probably need no explanation for the average hunter. Just in case someone runs across one that doesn't ring a bell, however, here they are: RMEF (Rocky Mountain Elk Foundation); SCI (Safari Club International); NRA (National Rifle Association); NAHC (North American Hunting Club); FNAWS (Foundation for North American Wild Sheep); and B&C (Boone and Crockett).

Finally, thanks to Ludo for assigning me this project. It is my fervent hope that *Ask the Elk Guides* will be received enthusiastically, and that every elk hunter on the planet will read it and find it useful. May God bless each of you, protect those close to you, and grant you the very finest elk hunting in the world.

Note to readers: J. Y. Jones can be reached at www.jyjones.com.

The author with the Manitoba elk that completed his collection of the four subspecies of North American elk.

Chapter 1

MEET THE ELK GUIDES

It is with great pleasure that I introduce elk hunters everywhere to perhaps the best assemblage of elk guides ever featured in one piece of literature.* From the youngest to the oldest, these guides are the most experienced group imaginable, and each has guided for an average of more than twenty-five years. Most are still actively outfitting and guiding, though a couple of them have ceased taking paying hunters and now hunt only for themselves. Whichever the case, all have a wealth of information to share, and what they have to say may open your eyes to a whole new world with respect to guide-client relations. I believe that anyone who has ever been guided on an elk hunt will find himself described somewhere in the pages of this book.

These guides share a large number of characteristics in common. They universally place a high premium on hunter ethics, honesty, integrity, hard work, patience, dependability, and persistence. They all desire their hunters to come well prepared in every possible way, and they go into great detail delineating how one goes about doing this. Despite the commonality of such thoughts, their individual words are unique and different, so the reader never gets bored.

These guides are truly excellent representatives of the outdoor fraternity, and I think you'll agree they all offer invaluable insights into the world of elk hunting. I can't think of a sufficient way to repay them for imparting their wealth of experience to us, the elk hunters of today, so thank them yourself when you see them . . . and enjoy these guys to the utmost!

*Each guide can be found here in the sequence they appear in the book, with a brief summary of their backgrounds and experience, contact information, and a recent photograph. The material included here is taken directly from interviews with the guides, and in some cases from printed material they supplied. Most information in this book has been obtained by means of telephone interviews with each guide, and is essentially as they said it.

Ask the Elk Guides

John Caid
White Mountain Apache Tribe
P.O. Box 220
White River, AZ 85941
928-338-4385
jcaid@wmonline.com

John Caid began guiding in 1979 as part of his job while working as biologist for the White Mountain Game and Fish Department. When the White Mountain Apache Tribe started a trophy elk hunt, John became interested in guiding hunters, and he is still at it. As of this writing, he has guided seventy-two hunters for trophy elk. He does it because of the excitement and the inherent challenge of the overall experience. He also enjoys meeting the hunters, and he says that the pay isn't bad, either! John reads "a ton of material" all the time. His favorite reading includes *Bugle*, *Sports Afield*, Garth Carter's publications, and *Petersen's Hunting*. John avidly reads virtually all of the hunting magazines, scanning them for whatever has to do with his favorite hunts—elk hunts in particular.

A jumble of fresh elk tracks.

Allen Morris
Three Forks Ranch
P.O. Box 69
Savery, WY 82332
970-583-7396
www.threeforksranch.com

Allen grew up on a Utah dairy farm and has been hunting all his life. In 1983, when he was sixteen, his father read an article in *Outdoor Life* about Wayne Carlton and his amazing diaphragm elk call, which was actually a turkey call. After a few false starts and phone calls to Wayne, who gave over-the-phone instructions, Allen learned to use the device. In his own words, "My life was changed forever." He began guiding friends and family immediately, calling in more than twenty bulls that fall, including bulls for himself and his father. In 1991 he began guiding elk hunters in northern Colorado, and afterward for eight seasons at the Slater Creek Ranch in Wyoming.

A few years ago he became a full-time elk guide and herd manager at Three Forks Ranch on the Colorado-Wyoming border. He won the 2003 Utah State Bugling Championship and was Northeast Elk Calling champion in 2002 and 2003. He has had several second- and third-place finishes at the World Elk Calling Championship. He has been guiding actively for twenty years and is still going strong. Allen has personally guided hundreds of elk hunters, and he says, "I've had my knife into over 550 elk." He guides because he loves to share the experience. When he went professional in 1991 it really changed his life again, because he got the chance to share his passion with a lot of different people from all over the country. He's a real lover of elk hunting, and if he's not out doing it, he's somewhere talking about it. Allen reads *Petersen's Hunting* and *Petersen's Bowhunting*, as well as RMEF's *Bugle*. He's a fan of Jim Zumbo and has read all of Jim's elk books.

Ask the Elk Guides

Jack Atcheson Jr.
Jack Atcheson & Sons
3210 Ottawa Street
Butte, MT 59701
406-782-2382/3498
www.atcheson.com

Jack became a guide of sorts when he was about thirteen, taking out some of his father's friends. People such as Jack O'Connor and other magazine writers came out every fall to hunt with them. Jack's earliest job was to drive around with hunters and show them the mountain ranges where they would be hunting.

He became a licensed guide at eighteen, and his first guiding experiences were for bighorn sheep. All those early hunters were licensed to hunt other species as well, and that's when Jack began to guide for elk. He ceased to guide in 2002, after being active for twenty-seven years; he has personally guided between 500 and 600 hunters. Jack guided because he couldn't get in enough hunting with his personal big-game tags, and he says that one elk tag for himself was never enough to satisfy his hunting passion. He wanted the experience of helping others take their elk, too.

For reading materials, Jack recommends that hunters read all the information that his company supplies regarding the camps and hunting situations. He notes that a lot of people don't understand what they're getting into when they book a hunt. One of the saddest things for him to hear reported is that a hunt wasn't what had been expected. He also recommends Jim Zumbo's books, which are directed toward the first-time elk hunter and can tell him what to expect while out hunting.

Chad Schearer
Central Montana Outfitters
P.O. Box 6655
Great Falls, MT 59406
406-727-4478
www.centralmontanaoutfitters.com

(Photo courtesy of Dusan Smetana)

Chad started guiding in 1991 in southwest Montana because he loved the outdoors and loved to hunt. He thought that guiding would be a great opportunity to spend more time out of doors. He has owned and operated Central Montana Outfitters since 1994. He still guides actively and has personally guided more than two hundred elk hunters. He looks upon elk hunting as an opportunity to get people out of doors and close to a bull elk. To him there's no more exciting feeling than to call in a bull elk for someone who has never hunted elk before, and to watch the new elk hunter harvest his first bull elk with bow or rifle.

Chad has been a speaker at some 350 elk hunting seminars around the country. He is an accomplished author and does a lot of writing for hunting periodicals. Among his favorite publications are *Outdoor Life* and the NRA's *American Hunter*. He enjoys the technical aspects of elk management and frequently reads scientific materials related to elk biology and habitat. He has been featured on a great many radio and television programs and also appears in many professional hunting videos. He is so accomplished at calling elk (and numerous other animals) that he has been featured as "the man who talks to the animals." He won the RMEF World Elk Calling championship in 1997 and has had numerous other first- and second-place finishes in major calling competitions.

Ask the Elk Guides

Van Hale
Trophy Outfitters
P.O. Box 1935
Eagar, AZ 85925
928-333-5290
www.trophyoutfittersonline.com

Van started outfitting professionally in 1981. Before that, when he was in high school, he often went down to the local restaurant and found hunters who hadn't scored yet and took them out to show them game. He has always been oriented to the outdoor life and has participated extensively in hunting and trapping.

He originally aspired to work for a game and fish department and attended college for a couple of years with that in mind. Instead, however, he decided that guiding was the path for him, so he started his own business in which he is both owner and a working guide. Van has guided between three- and four-hundred elk hunters in his career. While he enjoys the outdoors and hunting, and it's a way for him to be outdoors all the time, he also recognizes that his work provides his income.

One of the joys of his occupation is that he never has to look at a clock to see if it's starting or quitting time. He reads *Eastman's Journal*, among other hunting journals, because he believes that such publications give a truer than average perspective on hunting. He also particularly likes *Petersen's Bowhunting*.

Ross Johnson
Ross Johnson Outfitters
P.O. Box 26
Magdalena, NM 87825
505-772-5997
www.rossjohnson.com

Some twenty years ago, "kind of by accident," Ross started guiding hunters, using hounds to hunt bears. In the intervening years he has built a remarkable reputation as a guide who takes really big elk for his clients, and he still guides actively. Over the years he has guided hundreds of hunters for various species, including elk.

Guiding started out as an extension of his love for hunting. His operation has grown such that he has had to assume a lot more administrative and public relations duties, and he doesn't have time to guide as much as he did in the past—though he still does some each year.

He is an active pilot with thirty-five years of flying experience, and he uses that skill to scout new hunting areas, as well as for real estate work. Ross is notably straightforward, and he says with some disdain that he seldom reads any hunting publication. In his words, "If I pick up *Outdoor Life* or some of these other magazines and start reading an article, I get totally ticked off because the person who wrote it probably has no experience and doesn't know what he's talking about. So I just toss it down." That's Ross!

Ask the Elk Guides

Ron Dube
Ron Dube's Wilderness
Adventures
P.O. Box 167
Wapiti, WY 82450
307-527-7815
www.huntinfo.com/dube

Ron is known as the originator of modern elk calling contests. He initiated those contests in 1978 and wrote the original rules. He started outfitting in 1973, when he bought Caribou Resort in the Bighorn National Forest east of Buffalo, Wyoming. In order to extend his season, which was originally limited to the summer for tourists, he started guiding in the national forest for elk and on public and private land in the low country for deer and antelope. He's been doing it ever since and has specialized in horseback wilderness elk hunts since 1981. Ron still guides every day during hunting season, and he has guided hundreds of elk hunters over the years.

His motivation is personal satisfaction. While he recognizes that everybody has to do something for a living, he feels unusually blessed and fortunate to be able to do something that he truly enjoys. He states that he doesn't have time to read a lot of hunting magazines, but he does take pleasure in thumbing through *Big Game Adventures* as much as any publication. He also mentions *Petersen's Hunting*. Ron says that he is "not real wild" about *Outdoor Life*, *Field and Stream*, and *Sports Afield*, because he likes the old-fashioned me-and-Joe stories, along with profiles of individual people. He has a fascination, however, for letters to the editor. He most consistently scours RMEF's *Bugle*, which he always reads cover to cover. He is a life member of numerous hunter-conservationist organizations, including the RMEF, NRA, SCI, NAHC, and FNAWS.

Rick Trusnovec
Horse Creek Outfitters
P.O. Box 950
Challis, ID 83226
208-879-5400
www.hcoutfiters.com

It has been seventeen years since Rick began guiding professionally. He's originally from Long Island, New York, making his background unique among guides in this book, and probably rare among elk guides. He went to a guide/ packing school in 1986, and he's been active in the guiding industry ever since. He's guided about 200 hunters for elk, and at least that many for spring bear. His number one reason for guiding hunters is his love of the outdoors and the exhilaration of being out back in a wilderness area. According to him, such a life gets into your blood, no matter where you're from.

For him, it's unthinkable not to be in the backcountry in the spring and fall. Secondly, he really enjoys his clients, many of whom are tremendously interesting people. He likes to learn what his clients do for a living and how they got to where they are in life. He consciously uses down time while hunting in order to get to know people, and a lot of his clients become good friends. He reads *Petersen's Bowhunting* to stay up on archery hunting, and also RMEF's *Bugle*, as well as a host of other hunting publications. His partner, Jim Thomas, shares the business with Rick and has even more years of experience as a guide.

Ask the Elk Guides

Bob Fontana*
Elk Valley Bighorn Outfitters
P.O. Box 275
Cranbrook, BC,
Canada V1C 4H8
250-426-5789
www.lancasterfontana.com

The late Bob Fontana shot his first bull elk at sixteen. In 1977 he started guiding to help pay his way through the University of Calgary, where he earned a bachelor's degree in physical education. In those days he guided for outfitter Odd Aasland, and he took a seven-point bull with his very first guided client. For a couple of years he purchased spring grizzly rights to an area, and then in 1983 he purchased the entire area, at which point he retired from a brief career of teaching high school. He actively guided each hunter, and he once stated that he wouldn't be in the business if he couldn't go hunting himself. He enjoyed the activity of hunting and was particularly fond of hunting bighorn sheep, grizzly bears, and elk.

He was active in several other outfitting companies in British Columbia and the Northwest Territories of Canada. He was a founding member of the Outfitter Advisory Board of the RMEF, and a charter board member of RMEF Canada. He was named Outfitter of the Year in 2002 by the Guides and Outfitters Association of British Columbia. He read SCI's magazine *Safari*, RMEF's *Bugle*, and *The Hunting Report* regularly. He also read most of the other hunting magazines, such as *Trophy Hunter* and *Big Game Adventures*. He enjoyed old-time hunting books by people like Robert Ruark and Jack O'Connor. Bob became interested in outfitting after reading the works of Andy Russell, a Canadian writer who wrote *Grizzly Country* and *Horns in the High Country, stories* about packing into the high country.

*See tribute on page 168.

Readying the pack animals for the trip.

Wilderness packtrain into elk country.

Ask the Elk Guides

Brent Sinclair
Porcupine Creek Outfitters
P.O. Box 2442
Pincher Creek, Alberta,
Canada T0K 1WO
403-627-2540
brent@trophyhuntamerica.com

Brent grew up hunting, fishing, and trapping in rural Alberta. About 1973, Brent got interested in guiding when he met some people who had come to hunt bighorn sheep with Dave Simpson. Dave had a Western store in Pinchot Creek, Alberta, and Brent was fascinated to meet Dave's hunting clients. Brent found himself increasingly interested in guiding. After trying several less satisfying careers, he began guiding professionally in 1980, and he's still at it. He has personally guided between 800 and 1,000 hunters, of which some 275 to 300 were elk hunters.

He guides because he enjoys helping make a dream come true, and also to be in the country with the animals. For him it's a matter of personal satisfaction; it has far less to do with money and harvesting an animal. He notes that it's a way of life that can't be duplicated in any other line of work. He particularly enjoys the people he meets, the friends he makes, and the physical challenge. To Brent it's all worth it when he sees the smile of satisfaction on the face of someone who's had a dream come true.

Brent received the Outstanding Guide Award at the 2001 FNAWS Convention, recognizing his achievements within the way of life he cherishes so much. He reads *Wild Sheep*, *Safari*, *Big Game Adventures*, *Bowhunting*, *B.C. Hunter*, and many other periodicals. He likes to read magazines featuring people he knows, as these seem to be the ones that really give him insight into what's happening in the world of hunting. He also mentions *Shooting Times*, *Gun World*, and some others.

Dave Fyfe
North Island Guide Outfitters
2135 Nikola Place
Campbell River, BC,
Canada V9W 6H9
250-850-1500
www.huntingvancouverisland.com

Dave started guiding actively in 1982. Wayne Wiebe, the well-known outfitter on Vancouver Island, taught him well. Wiebe was looking for guides who were lifetime residents of Vancouver Island with knowledge of the area and its animals. Dave was fortunate to meet Wayne through his own personal deer and bear hunting, and the relationship developed from there. Although Dave now owns a substantial part of Wiebe's original guiding area, he still is a participating guide for both Roosevelt elk and black bear.

He admits that he has guided "not a ton" for elk. Vancouver Island is on a quota system for elk, and he is allowed only three permits per year in his area. Since 1994 when Dave took over a large portion of Wiebe's original area, they have had only twenty-seven permits and twenty-seven hunters. Dave also guided for Wayne Wiebe on several elk hunts. He has guided literally hundreds of black bear hunters; most seasons he personally guides twenty-five to thirty-five bear hunters. To Dave, guiding is a way of life, and he fully realizes that it is not likely to make him wealthy. There's a big commitment in time, being away from family, physical work, and so on. Dave enjoys knowing that he's living his dream, and the satisfaction that comes from being able to share with new people every year the love of the outdoors and the beauty of the land. He likes *Outdoor Life* and some of their good writers. He most enjoys reading about people's personal experiences with the thrill of the hunt.

Ask the Elk Guides

Bill Perkins
Wild Outdoor Adventures
32838 Old Bunker Hill Road
Saint Helens, OR 97051-9219
503-366-0233
billp@columbia-center.org

Bill started guiding when he was fourteen, partly for big game but mostly on charter boats along the Oregon coast. Bill is by far the most unconventional guide. He is not a professional elk guide, like the others presented here, since professional guides for Roosevelt elk hardly exist in the Washington-Oregon region. He has, however, more guiding experience for the Roosevelt subspecies than virtually anyone else in the Washington-Oregon area.

He enjoys taking people out for their first Roosevelt elk, and he has been successful in doing so on at least fifteen occasions. He has noticed that he often seems to get more excited than the hunter he is guiding, such is his joy at helping another person get an elk. While he usually takes family and friends hunting in Oregon, he is open to taking others as well, as long as killing an elk is not the overriding objective and as long as the hunter truly enjoys having a great time out-of-doors.

His resume is so inclusive that it is bewildering to try to condense it, but suffice to say that he has hunted extensively in many parts of the world. He and some partners are in the process of putting together a new hunting company (Wild Outdoor Adventures) that will have worldwide extension, with offices in more than a half-dozen countries and a Web site in six languages.

He belonged to the Oregon Guide and Packers Association for many years and still is a member of the Oregon Hunters Association. He is a life member of both SCI and the RMEF, and he is also active in many other hunter-conservationist

Elk camp.

organizations. Most of his big-game guiding nowadays occurs in New Zealand for all available big-game species there. He often reads SCI's *Safari* and RMEF's *Bugle*. His favorite books include the great classics on hunting in New Zealand and Africa.

Chapter 2
SELECTING AN OUTFITTER/ GUIDE FOR ELK

What should a hunter look for in an outfitter/guide?

John Caid: The first thing I'd look at is the quality of animals they have been taking. It's obvious that most hunters want to take the biggest animal they can. Second, I'd look at the guide's reputation among the hunters who have hunted with him. There are a lot of people who get into this business for one or two years and then are gone, so in my opinion, longevity should be a part of the equation. Every year when we go to the shows we see several brand new outfitters there. If they've been around a number of years, they're probably going to stay with it.

Allen Morris: In today's market, it's buyer beware when it comes to choosing an elk guide. You know, I hate to say that, but going across the country every year I encounter people that have been burned on an elk hunt. I think it's because they didn't do their background work. They didn't make the phone calls. A guide can put out a great brochure, he can tell you he's got the moon, and the stars to go with it, but unless you do the background work, unless you call every reference, and even call references you're given by the references, it's really buyer beware. There are guys out there offering a $2,000 to $3,000 elk hunt, and so many more hunters can afford that price than can afford one in the $6,000 range. A guy can get it by the wife a lot quicker if it's $2,500 than he can if it's five or six grand. In this industry I know there are some good outfits that run quality drop camps, and there are some good deals for $2,000 to $3,000, but you've really got to do your homework. Make those phone calls. Look at the references, and call the game department. They'll know if this guy's shady or not. All it takes is $30 to $40 on the telephone, and it might save you several thousand.

Jack Atcheson Jr.: In choosing a guide, I'd sure look at someone who's been in the business for some years. To me that's important. This is not a very lucrative field, and if they're in it for the long term, it's generally because they're successful and they understand what it takes to satisfy clients and keep everyone happy. I'd take a look at the areas they're hunting, too. I personally prefer wilderness area elk hunts, because to me that's what an elk hunt is all about. Still, there are certainly some good private land hunts popping up these days, as the elk population expands. Looking at areas and finding out the success ratio on mature bulls is important. Getting a five-year success ratio is probably the best indicator of what kind of success you might have, because that can change dramatically from year to year.

Chad Schearer: Hunters looking for a guide need to think about the type of hunt they want to go on, and how much they can afford. Not everybody can afford a $15,000 private land hunt in New Mexico. In some places you can still get a really good elk outfitter for $3,500 on up, or one could go even less expensive with a drop camp setup. Hunters need to find an outfitter who's going to cater to their needs. It depends on whether they're more a do-it-yourselfer, or if they want a fully guided experience, or whether they want to stay in a lodge at night and eat gourmet food. It just really depends on what type of hunter they are.

Van Hale: When it comes to choosing a guide, I think one of the most important things is experience, the track record, what the outfitter has been able to produce over the years. But an outfitter is only as good as his employees, since obviously your outfitter can't guide everybody. You might want to check on that aspect, to see if he has quality people working for him. If anyone ever has questions about me, I tell them to contact the local game and fish department and run a check. If a guy has a lot of violations, there's obviously some kind of problem. You also want to do some research on the areas that the outfitter is hunting.

Ross Johnson: What's important in a guide is a track record as far as what they've produced. It's very important how they've treated unhappy clients, particularly. I'd want to know whether or not they have been willing to refund hunt money when it's the outfitter's or guide's fault they had a bad experience. Integrity is important.

Ron Dube: In looking for a guide, I think the hunter should look for a quality reputation, plain and simple. Either the outfitter/guide has got the stuff, or he doesn't.

Rick Trusnovec: You can't do enough homework or ask enough questions when selecting a guide. You want to make sure the type of hunt you're going on will match your abilities and expectations. If you can't ride four or five hours on horseback to a camp through rough country, the guide and outfitter need to know that. You want to make a lot of phone

Elk hunting in the magnificent Selway-Bitterroot Wilderness.

calls, make sure the guy you want to hunt with is licensed, insured, and in good standing with the licensing board of the particular state where you're going to hunt. He should have a lot of references and be willing to hand over as many as a potential client wants, both successful and unsuccessful. A lot also depends on the type of hunter a guy is, whether he's strictly trophy hunting and is now looking only for a 330 or better bull. If that's the case, he's probably better off not coming with me.

When I go to a sport show, a guy may come to me after casing all the elk guides. Then he may come back and tell me he's been all around the show, and that my prices average a certain amount more than other guides, and he wants to know why. I'll ask him what kind of questions he asked. Did you ask how many hunters are in camp in a particular week? How many guides are run? Is there a cook and packer in camp? Sometimes they look at me a little funny. You know, a guy can sell a hunt for $1,000 cheaper than I can if he's running eight to ten hunters in a camp with five guides and no other help. I don't do that!

We try to educate the client on our side of things, so they can see how we do things. Say they book a two-on-one hunt with me, and they're paying $1,000 each more per week for the hunt. In most cases I run two guides and four clients in each camp. In each of my camps I have a full-time cook. If the other outfitter doesn't have a cook, then who does the cooking? Either the packer or the guide has to be the cook, too. There are a lot of outfitters who have the guide come back at night and do the cooking. Well, if I'm out there two hours away with two guys, and I'm looking at my watch thinking it'll be dark in two hours, then naturally I'm thinking, *Should I stay out here and hunt like I'm supposed to, or should I start working my way back to camp, because it's my turn to cook?* So you see, there's a lot more to it than meets the eye. If there's no packer in camp, the guide is going to do all the work of packing the animal back to camp. The other client, who hasn't killed anything, loses a whole day of hunting.

Of course, it's the client's responsibility to ask these questions, but the problem is that a lot of potential clients don't even know the questions to ask.

Bob Fontana: How to choose a guide is a tough question for an outfitter to answer. I think that honesty, integrity, and hard work are probably the standard answers you're going to get. That, and I'd also say a track record, but I don't want to walk on those guys who are just getting into the business. Everybody's got to start somewhere, right? So for that reason I'm a little reluctant to put high on my list what an outfitter's been doing. I like to see someone young and enthusiastic who's got a good area and wants to do a good job. I think they should get a fair crack at it. So now that I've been here a while I'm a little reluctant to say longevity, a track record, history, and the like.

Brent Sinclair: Look for an individual who's going to be honest in providing answers. If you're looking to harvest a 400-class elk, the outfitter should be honest enough to tell you if he can't provide that. Look for someone who's going to be able to provide the experience and the quality of service that you're looking for as a hunter. Above all, look for someone who's honest enough to tell you if he can deliver the hunt you expect.

Dave Fyfe: The hunter needs to look for the guide/outfitter who can help him achieve his personal goals. If I were trying to choose someone that I'd go hunting with, my approach would be to set my goal first by deciding what it is I want out of the hunt. Am I looking for a monster trophy? Do I want to have an easy hunt? Do I want to look at large numbers of animals? After I decide those questions, I choose an outfitter that can help me achieve my goals.

Bill Perkins: The first thing is to ask how long the guide has been in business in the area you want to hunt. Also, what is his success rate? I know good moose guides that also guide for grizzly, and yet they may not really know what they're doing when it comes to bears. So make sure the outfitter/guide is good at hunting what you want. References only go so far, and remember that outfitters will sometimes

Glassing for elk; evidence in the foreground proves they've been here!

give you only the best ones. Hunt reports available through SCI and other sources are a great tool in finding outfitters and guides.

What is the most important single characteristic of a good guide?

John Caid: Persistence, staying with it, and not giving up. There are a lot of days as a guide that you get frustrated. I think this applies not only to guiding but to other professions as well. You've got to be persistent and have the ability to keep on going while maintaining a good attitude, even under the worst of circumstances.

Allen Morris: The first characteristic I look for is being a great hunter. But great hunters don't always make great guides. The best guides are good people-people. A great guide has got to be as excited about the client getting an animal as he would be about getting one for himself. If you're a great hunter with excellent people skills, and you take care of your client while he's on the mountain, that makes you a great guide. I can't imagine what I would do in a hardwood swamp in Alabama or Georgia where I couldn't see a reference, but some guys come out here and get lost even looking at the mountains. They're so awestruck that they really need to have confidence in their guide's abilities. It's people skills, being excited for the client, and being a good hunter.

Jack Atcheson Jr.: Patience.

Chad Schearer: The most important characteristic is people skills. I've noticed that some of the best elk hunters in the world would likely make some of the worst guides. I'd rather have a guide working for me who is only a good elk hunter but can really get along well with people. A guide with no people skills isn't much good to an outfitter, even if he's a super elk hunter. A hunter is going to spend anywhere from five to seven days with the guide, and it really helps if he can get along with him, work with him, solve problems with him, and so on. So people skills are most important. After that, it's understanding elk and understanding hunting them.

Van Hale: A good guide must be able to communicate with the client—be able to show that he knows what he's doing so he gains the client's confidence. It has to do with people skills. There are a lot of good hunters out there, but not a lot with top-quality people skills. If the guide and the hunter are on the same page, chances of success are greatly improved.

Ross Johnson: To me a good guide is one who's willing to go the extra mile to get his hunter an opportunity.

Ron Dube: Being aggressive and success-oriented makes a good guide. I also think that experience is important. We have six to eight guides during the fall, some for only a week or two, though most work for me all fall. The majority of them have been with me for years. Some of them are people who have owned their own business in other parts of the country for ten to fifteen years or more. As one of their annual vacations they come out and guide a few hunts for me. Many of them are former clients.

Rick Trusnovec: I can't give you just one characteristic of a good guide, but knowledge of elk is important, as well as knowledge of the area. Second would be personality. You've got to have a good personality to click with your client. You can't just go out and sit on a hillside for fifteen hours a day and not speak or communicate. You've got to quietly visit with your client to get to know him, and that's part of the whole picture.

Bob Fontana: Ability is what's important in a guide. That's an all-encompassing kind of characteristic, and it depends some on the area you're going to be hunting. The old-time, wilderness-type pack-in hunts that we still conduct require a more diverse set of abilities than some of the other elk hunts that are available, particularly some of the private land hunts, which are conducted primarily by four-wheel-drive vehicle. Ability covers four or five areas that are going to be important, but primarily elk hunting skills, such as the ability to glass, bugle, locate elk, and think like an elk. In our area horsemanship skills are important. Knowledge of the area you're hunting is a big thing, and being willing to put in a hard day's work. Then you get into some of the social skills. So ability is a fairly all-encompassing answer to this question.

Brent Sinclair: A good guide must be able to keep an individual's momentum moving forward, and to keep a positive attitude, even when things aren't going so well. When hunts go tough and the weather's not working and the game is hard to find, you need to be able to keep a positive attitude and relate that to the hunter. The client must never lose the feeling that he's going to have his opportunity.

Dave Fyfe: What makes a good guide? Every time I finish a hunt and I feel the hunter has had a great time, it's because I or one of my guides have been a really good companion for him. Not only is a good guide a good companion, he is also a good teacher. He's got to have an intimate knowledge of both the area they're hunting and the animals they're hunting to do this. Obviously success is important, but if a person has come and learned a lot about the area and the animals,

Big elk can live in thick country.

and he's had a good time, I think you can say he's been with a good guide.

Bill Perkins: A good guide is able to deal with all types of people and adapt the hunt to what is working on that day. Also, good communications are key to a successful hunt, so guides should be good communicators.

What is the worst possible deficiency in a guide?

John Caid: Dishonesty. In this profession there are a lot of fly-by-night outfitters who will take your money and then do a bait and switch. They sell you something, and when you show up it's totally a different deal.

Allen Morris: The biggest deficiency in a guide, assuming he's an adequate hunter, is that he's just there to make money. He doesn't take the time to explain why they're doing what they're doing, nor even the difference between a patch of quakies and a patch of pines—the details of the hunt. He won't explain things because he's really not there for the hunter; he's there for himself. I think that's a glaring deficiency with a lot of Western guides, unfortunately. There are some great hunters out there who are lousy guides. And there are probably some good guides who are lousy hunters, but they're great with people and they do all right.

Jack Atcheson Jr.: The worst deficiency in a guide is impatience.

Chad Schearer: Having a substance abuse problem is the worst. I've been in camps where guys like to party a little too much, and it really cuts time off their elk hunt. The problem in such cases is too much alcohol at the wrong time.

Van Hale: Laziness. If a guy is lazy, the hunters will pick up on that and feel they aren't getting a fair shake. Basically, a guide should be able to hunt as hard as the hunter wants to. In my opinion, the guide should be in as good shape as the client, or better, and he should have a much greater knowledge of the area and its game. If he's lazy, he won't have any of those characteristics.

Ross Johnson: The worst guide is the one who's there just for the paycheck. For him, it's just another routine, another week. He doesn't take any interest in the hunter, because all he wants is the money.

Ron Dube: The worst deficiencies in a guide are not being aggressive enough, being less than knowledgeable about the craft, and being lazy. If a guide is not willing to get out there and hustle, obviously he's not going to take the time to learn his craft well.

Rick Trusnovec: The opposite of what I said before: not knowing the elk and not knowing the area, and having no personality. If a guy hasn't a clue out in the field, he's handicapped and can never develop a decent relationship with the client.

Ask the Elk Guides

Bob Fontana: The worst guide is someone who is a braggart or pretends he's someone he's not. Watch out for the guy who makes a lot of noise when you first meet him but then can't deliver.

Brent Sinclair: Laziness is the worst deficiency. It makes for a tough hunt every time.

Dave Fyfe: Having poor judgment. That's fairly far-reaching, but a good guide can look at a hunter and soon assess his ability and experience. A poor guide can be a poor judge of his hunter, and as well he might be a poor judge of the animals he's hunting.

Bill Perkins: The worst deficiency is impatience! I've seen guides make a hunt go sour because they don't have the patience to deal with certain kinds of people.

Chapter 3

THE ELK GUIDES EVALUATE THE HUNTER

What is your favorite type of hunter?

John Caid: I think that my favorite type of hunter has a good personality and a willingness to hunt hard. We've guided since 1979, and I've found that physical ability and most other individual attributes are not that critical. I like someone who comes in and says, "Let's go have a good time. I'm here because I love to hunt. Let's go have fun for the next seven days and look for the biggest bull we can find." That's my favorite kind of hunter.

Allen Morris: A lot of factors go into choosing a favorite type of hunter. I like a personality that's easygoing and that takes adversity in stride . . . someone who exemplifies the expression "Like water off a duck's back." When it comes to physical ability, I've had them all—guys in wheelchairs, even a quadriplegic who pulled the trigger with his mouth. Physical ability is second to their expectations. It doesn't matter if the hunter is a rocket scientist or a guy who hangs sheetrock, as long as he's set up psychologically for an elk hunt. There are so many guys who come out here, and if they don't shoot a big 6x6 bull they're disappointed. Well, who gave them that expectation? Was it their own, or did the outfitter tell them something like, "We shoot nothing but six-pointers."

My favorite type of hunter might come from anywhere or any background. The kind of hunter I like has an affable personality, easily deals with adversity, such as rain, snow, flat tires, and things like that. Physical ability is secondary to personality and how the hunter looks at a hunt.

Jack Atcheson Jr.: If your hunter is fidgeting and nervous, you can see you're in for trouble. A lot of hunters I've taken out over the years were ready to go home within half a day. They

Elk country.

couldn't wind down and start hunting and leave the office behind. That's back to patience again. When you're hunting wild animals, the animal doesn't really care how much money you've spent on the hunt. You've got to rise to the level of the animal you're hunting. Sometimes it takes a few days or a few weeks to get there. Elk hunters need to be at least of moderate physical ability. They need to be able to get there. They don't need to be fast, they just need to be able to get there eventually, and just hang in. That's persistence again. Money isn't a necessity, but it helps if it isn't a critical factor. In hunting elk a lot of times you're not going to get one on the first trip, or the second.

Chad Schearer: My favorite type of hunter is the one who comes on an elk hunt for the experience and the essence of the hunt. There are a lot of people who come into camp and say, "I paid $4,000 for this elk hunt, and I expect to kill an elk." Well, we're all out there because we want everybody to get an elk. But elk are one of the hardest big game species to harvest, so a person needs to have the right frame of mind.

40

Physical conditioning is good, but mental conditioning is just as important. A person might travel 3,000 miles or more to go on an elk hunt, and when he gets there he finds 3 feet of snow on the ground and a temperature of 30 below zero—and the elk just aren't moving. Or there may be 80-degree temperatures and the elk are moving after dark, becoming nocturnal. These are factors the outfitter can't control, and I really like a hunter who's able to accept this without complaining. A hunter must go elk hunting with the idea of having the best time possible, and that harvesting an animal is just a bonus. I want to be careful, though, that people don't get the idea that I'm not serious, or that we don't really want them to harvest an elk. That is what I'm after, but you have to look at the big picture.

Van Hale: My favorite hunter is the guy who comes out here to hunt, and he doesn't already have the animal mounted in his mind before he gets here, just because he paid for the hunt. He's really coming to enjoy the outdoors and the experience of the hunt. It's the goal for all of us to kill an elk, but my kind of hunter is the guy who enjoys himself whether he kills an elk or not.

Ross Johnson: I like a hunter who has been there and done that, like the man who wants a 400-class bull. I like it if he's taken big animals before, so he knows what he's asking for. I don't like the guy who thinks he's entitled to kill a big elk because he's paid the dollars. The guy who has experience knows what he's asking for, and that it might not come easy. Ideally, a hunter should have experience plus physical abilities.

Ron Dube: I like people who are serious about hunting and getting their game, and are willing to pass up smaller elk if they want a big one. If a guy wants to shoot a smaller elk—say, he's never killed one before—I'm happy to accommodate him. I don't care how much money a person has. I like people with a positive attitude who are willing to put up with a little adversity, maybe a little weather, maybe some physical discomfort, so they can have a good overall wilderness experience. Whiners and complainers are not my cup of tea.

Ask the Elk Guides

Rick Trusnovec: My favorite type of hunter is in basically good shape. He doesn't have to be a marathon runner, but I like it if he can get around the hill and do some walking when necessary. I like them quiet, and I like them to listen to what I have to say. If and when an opportunity is getting close, the kind of hunter I like really pays attention. In this business, you're either the elk guru or the elk idiot. If I'm dealing with new clients, my idea is to educate them. A lot of them are very willing to listen to what I have to say, but there are also some who expect things to happen exactly according to their expectations; if circumstances cause things to go differently, they lose all confidence in me, and I become the idiot to them. The general quality of hunters has definitely started to go downhill, because there are a lot of hunters coming out who are over forty and never did any hunting as a kid. The basic skills just aren't there, and that really hurts out in the field. We try to explain the dos and don'ts, and some listen, some don't.

Bob Fontana: I like folks who have come out to experience the total nature of the hunt. They're booking a hunt with me to see the Rockies in their fall splendor, to listen to elk bugle, and to participate in an old-fashioned, free-ranging elk hunt. My favorite type of hunter is the dedicated elk hunter that likes to hunt elk every year, and likes to go on horseback and ride into those high basins, and do it for all the right reasons.

I'm not trying to put myself off the hook for producing bulls, but I find that the guys who come here for the enjoyment of the trip and to hear the elk bugle and to see the Rockies when they're the most majestic, those guys tend to do the best anyway. They are the ones who aren't worried about how big a bull they're going to get and how it's going to score, or on what day they're going to get it. I guess the guys that aren't in a big hurry, who are there to enjoy the country and the effort we put forth, are also my favorites. I like them to be in as good shape as they can possibly be, but they don't have to be superstars.

Brent Sinclair: I really like someone who comes in with a positive attitude and doesn't have unrealistic expectations of the guide. I like a good sense of humor. I like someone who understands that hunting is hunting, and it contains an element of uncertainty. As long as the guide gives a good, honest effort, the client who provides that same kind of effort has my vote. It's important that the hunter has the ability to work with the guide to gain a great experience.

Dave Fyfe: I prefer a hunter who clearly enjoys all aspects of the hunt. He hasn't hung his hat so much on killing the animal as on meeting the guide, getting to know the area, learning about the animals, and the like. I like to watch how he uses a camera. When I see a guy taking a lot of pictures—some of the rubs and plants, scenery shots—I know he is savoring every part of the hunt. That to me shows he's really enjoying the experience. Those are some of my favorite types of hunters.

Bill Perkins: My favorite is the person who enjoys being in the woods. If he gets an animal, that is just the icing on the cake. I believe some people try too hard. They measure their success entirely on what animal they took and how large it is. I believe in the camaraderie of the hunt. I really enjoy getting to know someone and imparting to them skills that have helped me be successful in my own hunting.

What is the most challenging type of hunter, and why?

John Caid: Hunters can be challenging of your skills or your temperament. It's certainly a challenge getting people who aren't physically in shape to take an elk. We have twenty-nine guides who work under me, and I stress to them that you can only do what your hunter can do. If he can't get up that hill, you've got to find a different way to hunt that elk. Or you've got to take him to another area that's easier. There are certainly other challenges. We have hunters who come to White Mountain Apache Reservation because of its reputation. Some of them will say, "I know you know where the big ones are. I know you've got one 'tied up,' so let's cut the crap. Take me straight to that bull and don't drag me around for five days." That guy's not here to enjoy the hunt. He's here just to harvest the biggest bull in Arizona and get out. A hunter with that kind of attitude is probably more challenging than a person with a lack of physical ability. I'll take a hunter with less physical ability and a great attitude over the other kind any day.

Allen Morris: The most challenging hunter is the one with really high expectations. He considers himself a trophy hunter, or for some reason nothing but a 6x6 that scores over 330 will do. I've got the best elk hunting anywhere on the Three Forks Ranch, but the flip side is that I don't have a lot of really big bulls. I can show a guy fifty to a hundred bulls a day, but most of them will be 4x4s or 5x5s, with the occasional six-pointer. So the most challenging type of hunter is the one who puts heavy-duty expectations on himself and the guide. You can try to mold their expectations, but it's challenging to deal with

Searching the high country.

some of these type-A personalities that have to do it their way. I've had to tell some guys, "Hey, look, you're paying a lot of money to have my expertise. If you want to run the hunt, that's fine. But you're going to have to listen to me eventually, and then we'll be successful."

Jack Atcheson Jr.: A misinformed hunter is the biggest challenge because you have to spend the first part of the trip educating and training your man. For instance, you get a man who comes in and says, "I want a 370-point bull elk, and that's all I'll shoot." Immediately, in order to allow him to enjoy most hunting areas, you're going to have to tell him the odds of killing a bull in that class, how many of them there are, and the like. For instance, in Yellowstone, which is an unhunted population of elk, 4 percent of the elk are four-pointers or better. So if you translate that to areas where there is hunting, the chances of killing any six-point bull is low unless there's pretty aggressive management going on. If a guy has unrealistic expectations, he's setting himself up for a fall.

Chad Schearer: The most challenging hunter is someone who does not have realistic expectations. Hunting elk in the wild is not hunting a game farm. If you spook elk they can move 8, 10, or even more miles. A challenging hunter is one that comes and says, "That's not how they do it on television. That's not how they do it on video." I do television and video, and I've got a half-hour show. It may take you seven to ten days to get the footage you need. It's really challenging if people don't have the right expectations.

Van Hale: It's a big challenge when you have a guy who automatically thinks he's going home with an animal, and if he doesn't the hunt is ruined for him. He puts too much pressure on himself and his guide to kill something, and he just doesn't relax and enjoy himself. It's a mental thing, and it can hurt the whole camp.

Ross Johnson: Two kinds of hunter are probably the most challenging: One is the guy who's handicapped by his smoking habits and is overweight and can't get around. A lot of times he's a really nice guy and you want him to be successful, but it's tough. And then there's the guy who seems to be totally unlucky as far as elk are concerned. No matter what you seem to do or who he hunts with, he can't get his animal.

Ron Dube: Probably the most challenging hunter is the fellow who has a big ego and pushes his weight around, who expects rules and laws and regulations to be bent to accommodate him. Braggarts and loudmouths are also hard to take.

Another type of person, one that's not so abrasive, is the one who's just totally unfit for the rigors of the outdoors. It's quite a challenge for a guide to take such a guy on a physically demanding wilderness elk hunt if he just doesn't have the physical ability to get the job done.

And then there are some that just can't shoot. Gee, whiz, I had a guy one time that missed five different easy shots at bulls— and he was a custom gunmaker!

Rick Trusnovec: The most challenging hunter is the guy who's hunted elk for a lot of years on his own and feels like he knows everything about elk hunting. For some reason, however, he decides to get into a wilderness setting where he's got a better chance of harvesting a bigger bull than he's ever taken, so he goes out and books with an outfitter. When he comes in, he wants to tell me how it ought to be done. He's a know-it-all. That doesn't work in my camp. If I get tested or pushed enough by such a person, my fall-back is to ask, "How many years have you been elk hunting?"

He may say thirty or thirty-five years. I then ask, "How many bulls have you taken?"

I've never had anybody say more than eight or ten. I then tell him that in just the last two seasons, I've killed more than twenty bulls with clients. That will often end the discussion— but not always.

Bob Fontana: For me the biggest challenge is hosting the hunter who is in a hurry, the one who's here only for a big elk, not for the experience. It's the kind of guy who books a ten-day, one-on-one elk hunt, gets here, and then wants to be home in three days. He immediately wants to know where his 350 or 360 bull is, and how he can get it really quick. I guess it's the

Selway-Bitterroot elk camp.

guys whose bad hunt turns into a good hunt only when their 3,200 feet per second happens.

Brent Sinclair: Someone who is always second-guessing his guide and always questioning his decisions is a major challenge to me.

Dave Fyfe: The guy who is not mentally prepared for the hunt can be the biggest challenge. There are lots of things tied in with that. As an example, take a guy coming to hunt with us on Vancouver Island. This is a wet environment, a coastal rain forest. It can feel like standing in a cold shower all day. If a guy is not prepared for that, he sets himself up for disappointment.

It's also tough when the hunter is not prepared for the hunt, hasn't considered that there is some physical exertion involved, or that there may be long periods when we don't see any game. Sometimes guys who aren't mentally prepared come around during the hunt, and during the time with us they get over the shock of finding out that this isn't the Serengeti and there isn't

47

big game on every hill. They are fine after that. But if they don't get over it, they can be a real challenge.

Bill Perkins: The most challenging kind of hunter is the person that has to have an animal and doesn't care what it takes. The fun of the hunt is thrown away, and when it is over it was no big deal to them. I believe that you should enjoy just being out there and seeing the animals in their natural surroundings.

How do you handle the inexperienced hunter? The physically challenged hunter?

John Caid: Inexperienced hunters first. We have a lot of hunters who have never heard an elk bugle, or maybe have a little experience but have not seen a big bull. We usually take them out the night before to an area where I know the elk are going to be bugling, and we'll sit there and let them listen for the evening. Then we'll go back to camp.

Our hunts are seven days long, and I tell them we're going to look for a record-book elk for about four days. The first couple of days we're going to look at bulls, and unless one's an absolute monster we're not going to shoot. We're going to look at those bulls, and I'm going to tell you what's good about them and what's bad. For example, a bull walks out and it's got great eye guards, and if it goes past the nose it's going to be sixteen inches long. We'll go through the things that make that bull weak— maybe spread or mass. The first few days we go over that with them as we're looking at elk. By the third or fourth day they should be picking it up, telling me, "Hey, that one's got good third points," and so on. I try to tell the inexperienced hunter why we do certain things, why we're hunting a certain area, and why we're turning down a particular bull. I try to make it more enjoyable and get the hunter more involved in the hunt.

As for the physically challenged hunter, we try to determine ahead of time if a hunter has any physical condition that we need to know about—whether it's high blood pressure, a heart condition, a bum knee, or a weight problem. If they can't get up and down the mountain, we might take them to a meadow or find a flat place to hunt. We try to work with them and figure out what they can and can't do. We also run the Havasupai Reservation, where it's fairly flat, so we might take them there. We don't press them too hard, particularly in the first couple of days. If a guy feels he's done, we take him in, even if it's 7:00 A.M. If they just can't get around, we'll hunt them over a watering place or a big meadow. Sometimes we take them to the top of the mountain where we know the elk go to bed down, and we'll wait up there for the animals to come.

Jack Atcheson Jr.: With an inexperienced hunter, you just have to be patient and explain the reasons why you're doing things. You tell him we're going to watch the wind currents in this drainage: They blow up in the morning, so we can't go in until the afternoon. You've got to explain your actions to that man so he doesn't become puzzled or unhappy that things aren't working out the way they do in the *Outdoor Life* stories he's read. You've got to take time to educate him. If you're working

It's cold and it's snowy, but there's an elk up there.

with an experienced old whitetail hunter, he will pick right up on it, and even share some of his own experiences, which will make it a better trip. As for the physically challenged, you've got to recognize that there are two types of hunters: one capable of doing the bayonet charge, and another who relies on stealth and cunning. There are places where a guy can sit and watch and just be patient; someone who's physically challenged can use patience to his advantage. He will often kill as big an animal as someone who wants to be a roadrunner.

Chad Schearer: I've guided both inexperienced and physically challenged hunters. Basically, you help a person as much or as little as he needs. For some hunters, pretty much all I do is go with them, like hunting with a buddy. For others, you have to make sure their gun is unloaded, and even that it's sighted in. Some people you just have to help more than others. You simply have to read the hunter when he shows up. For the physically challenged hunter, you have to hunt in areas where he can get around. That kind of hunter has to understand that, because he is challenged, it can be a little more difficult to achieve success, even though we do everything humanly possible to make it happen.

Van Hale: Inexperienced hunters are actually some of my favorite people to guide. Because they are inexperienced they are easier to teach, and they will usually do what you say in the field. I enjoy hunting with those guys. Before each hunt we have a safety meeting, and we detail how the client is to handle his gun. We have some other rules, too, such as not having a round in the chamber until the guide tells you to put one in. The handicapped hunter can be tough, depending on what kind of hunt he wants. Over in New Mexico, for example, they have a lot of hunts that are open only to handicapped people, and you have a separate set of rules—such as its being legal to shoot from a vehicle and the like.

Ross Johnson: The inexperienced hunter is not a problem, because we mail out a questionnaire asking what they've hunted before, and we try to match up their experience level with the right guide and the right camp situation. The physically handicapped hunter is a real challenge. It helps that we use tree stands, ground blinds, and the like, but we make it clear that his chance of success is lower. We don't get too many physically challenged hunters, because most of our hunters are high-profile guys who know what they want, and the hunts are sometimes pretty tough.

Ron Dube: The inexperienced hunter is easy to handle, especially if he has a positive image of his outfitter and guide, because you can coach him. And ladies are like that. We've taken lots of lady hunters that didn't have much experience, but they were willing to learn and follow the recommendations of their guide. I had a lady one time that thought the elk was too far away, and I said, "No, he's not too far away." I got her a very secure rest and told her where to put the cross hairs; she killed that elk. As for the physically challenged, they are not as difficult to accommodate as one would think, if they have a good attitude. We take a lot of older people and people with bad knees, and I understand that not everyone is an Arnold Schwarzenegger. We tailor the hunt according to the physical abilities of the client. As long as they can ride a horse, we can take them to a lot of places that they would be unable to get to otherwise. We've been quite successful, and we've had a lot of clients in that category kill good bulls.

Rick Trusnovec: Inexperienced elk hunters are often the best hunters. People who know they don't know anything are far better than people who think they know all about it. They look up to you; they want to know what to do. You don't have to go back and repeat a lot of things to the inexperienced hunter. As much as I enjoy my repeat hunters, the inexperienced hunter is the most pleasant person to deal with on an elk hunt. Inexperience can be a plus, as I see it. The physically handicapped person, however, is really difficult for us, working in a wilderness setting. We can take handicapped hunters, but they've got to be able to ride horseback. We do the best we can for them, taking them to places where elk cross, or where they can glass. We really need to know up front what the handicap is, so we can let them know if we can offer them a good experience.

Ask the Elk Guides

Bob Fontana: We get quite a lot of inexperienced hunters. All my clients participate in a warm-up session to let them know what it's going to be like. We're a little bit different here in B.C., in that we can hunt elk with rifles during the peak of the rut. A lot of the rifle hunters we get aren't used to that nose-to-nose confrontation, so we have a two-hour seminar the first day of the hunt in which we talk about what it may be like. We go over gun safety, horsemanship, and then we get right into the placement of shots. We start with diagrams, then we use horses as stand-ins for elk so we can demonstrate exactly where to shoot. We try to walk them through every aspect of the hunt. I like to sit down and talk to all the hunters and guides who will be going out, and go through all the details of hunting elk during the rut. I'm a former schoolteacher, so I don't mind standing up in front with a chalkboard and walking through the process.

For us, the physically challenged would mean simply people who aren't in good shape. For the truly physically handicapped, because of our setting it would be hard for us to do much in that regard. We match our clients to both the country and the guide, because we have some country that's softer than the rest. We put those older hunters or those not in tip-top shape in places where they don't have to be all that tough to get in a good ten-day hunt.

Brent Sinclair: Inexperience requires explanation of your game plan, and that you communicate what your next move will be. You've got to try to keep an inexperienced hunter from being surprised by your next decision. Explain what you'll be doing if the animal does such and so, and what the alternatives are. Continue to provide information on your game plan and let him know what comes next. You need to communicate what you're doing and what to expect next, and do it every few hours or at least a couple of times a day, so there are no surprises. For the physically challenged, you've simply got to gear yourself to the physical abilities of the hunter. You don't take a physically challenged person into some of the more rugged country and expect him to keep up. You should be able to work with the conditions and the terrain so that the client can have a quality hunt based on what he is capable of doing.

Dave Fyfe: The inexperienced hunter needs a good teacher. Sometimes we have to start with the most basic things, after we assess a guy's ability. For example, if he's not experienced using his binocular, we teach him the fine points. If he's not all that comfortable with his rifle, we don't get him out in the bush in front of an elk before we start talking to him about performing with his rifle.

As for the physically challenged, we do get many, although more on our bear hunts than our elk hunts. We have 2,700 square miles in our area, and we have a wide variety of terrain in which we can hunt. I ask my guides to match the hunter's physical ability with the terrain. It's something we have to discuss with the hunter, too, even if it's uncomfortable. You've got to get to the bottom of a person's ability, because nobody wants to kill anybody on the mountain. It's the responsibility of the guide and outfitter to make that assessment. It may be that a

An awesome bull elk can make even the most experienced hunter shiver with excitement!

guy can't get to some of the areas that are difficult to reach, and consequently some trophy animals will not be available to him. Creating an enjoyable hunt is the main thing, and putting someone through a hellish experience certainly doesn't contribute toward that.

Bill Perkins: When I take out inexperienced hunters, I spend time teaching them the basics. We cover listening, seeing, smelling—all the things you need for a successful elk hunt. I talk to them about where we are and what to do if we were separated or some other trouble arose. How would they get out of the woods? I watch how they hold their gun and how they test fire it. Do they flinch or jerk, things that could make them miss? Are they scared of the gun? Does it kick too much? I want them to feel very comfortable in the woods, as if they could do the hunt on their own if they had to. Most people who start out hunting elk have a hard time seeing the animals. I work with them on what to look for in the woods. What looks out of place? I instruct them on how elk use the woods and where you might find them in certain terrain. I try to teach beginners all the basics of being a good hunter, but of course it doesn't happen overnight. I have little experience guiding physically challenged hunters.

What type of hunter do you most dislike guiding? Is there any particular characteristic that would make you refuse to guide a hunter?

John Caid: A couple of things would make me refuse to guide a hunter. The first would be if he's totally irresponsible with his firearm—if he's waving it around, pointing it at people, or just can't get it under control. I'd refuse to guide him, and I would give him his money back. Second, if a hunter tries to offer me more money to shoot another bull or something else that is unethical or illegal, my first inclination is to take him immediately back to camp. I tell my guides that they can put up with almost anybody for seven days, but hunter safety and personal safety are extremely important. If one of our guides finds himself hunting with a client who is dangerous with a firearm, he can end the hunt. The same goes for illegal offers.

Allen Morris: There's no single situation that would always make me end a hunt. I'm in the business of taking people out and showing them elk hunting. There are always guys in camp, of course, who say that the lights aren't bright enough, the food's not good enough, the cabin's drafty, and—even if you've got the best elk hunting in the world—the bulls aren't big enough. I don't think those guys are happy about anything, but they've paid their money to hunt. I may dislike them, but I know for a fact that I can live with the Devil himself for five days. I just don't let them get me down. I focus on the task at hand, which is taking them out and calling in as many elk as I can and letting them make the decisions. If a hunter refuses to shoot the first bull or the last bull, or if I call in two hundred bulls and he doesn't shoot, it's his hunt. To a degree I let them all dictate the way the hunt goes for them. All I can do is put them in front of the elk and hope that a little good fortune shines on us both.

Jack Atcheson Jr.: I hate to guide a know-it-all. They can be a problem. Maybe I've got a repeat hunter, and we saw a big bull someplace last year. Until I take him to that very place and show him that the same big bull isn't there, we can't hunt anywhere else! Every area is different, and elk act differently in every region. One hunter may know all about hunting elk in New Mexico, but if he goes up to British Columbia the rules of the game are going to be a little different. Listening to the guide is important. I've guided for lots of elk, but if I go on a guided hunt myself, I hire a good man and fall right in behind him and let him do his thing. As for refusing to guide a hunter, I don't like hard drinkers. I'd decline if I knew about that. I think you need to leave the booze out of the hunting camp. I don't like to hunt with quitters, or with people who don't hunt from daylight until dark when conditions are right. Why would you book a ten-day hunt and not hunt for ten days, unless you get your elk? If people have a bad attitude, they can stay at home. Disagreeable people ought not to be in a hunting camp.

Ask the Elk Guides

Chad Schearer: I most dislike guiding somebody who is there just to make a kill, and who is unappreciative of the time and effort it takes to put in the camps, do the scouting, and all the rest. That is the type of guy who just takes everything for granted. All he's there for is to kill an elk, and if he doesn't kill one he's not happy. I'd refuse to guide a hunter who wants to drink while we're out hunting. As an outfitter you learn to put up with a lot, and that's part of the business, but if a hunter just can't get along with anyone I wouldn't guide him again. The other thing that would make me refuse to guide is if someone wanted to do something illegal.

Van Hale: I most dislike it when a guy walks up to me at a show and asks if I will guarantee him an animal, or if I'll guarantee that such-and-such will happen on a hunt. There are no guarantees when it comes to hunting. If you want a guaranteed animal, go to a game farm. It makes me put a red flag beside that guy's name, because he's probably already had a lot of bad experiences. You're not going to be able to please him. If a guy is unsafe in the field, or lacks respect for the animal we're hunting, I'd probably refuse to guide him again.

Ross Johnson: I hate guiding the person who has too much of an attitude, who feels like he's paying for the animal, who has no respect for the animal. There have been two or three of those hunters who have taken 400-class bulls, and I've regretted they did. Their lack of respect showed me that they didn't deserve the elk, and that elk ought not to have died by their hands. I really dislike people who have no respect for the animal they're hunting. It's that kind of attitude that would definitely make me refuse to have a hunter back to my camp.

Ron Dube: Boy, you're putting me on the spot there. It's an outfitter's job to accommodate all of his clients, and they come in all different shapes, colors, sizes, and attitudes. I don't like guiding people who are obnoxious and disrespectful of others, but I can put up with them. Physical ability has nothing to do with it. I ended a guy's hunt one time because he was in camp swearing in front of the women. I asked him not to use that kind of language and he got even worse, so I ended his hunt. He won't be coming back hunting with me.

Rick Trusnovec: I can't take it when a guy is looking for a guaranteed hunt in our wilderness setting. I never have guaranteed an elk, and I never will. It's absolutely out of the question, because of the place and circumstances under which we hunt.

Bob Fontana: Because of the nature of the places we hunt, I don't like to book someone who has expectations of a certain score on a bull. I'll definitely take someone hunting who wants to look for the biggest bull he can find—that doesn't bother me. But when somebody tells me that he expects to shoot a 350- or 360-point bull, I just won't go down that trail.

Brent Sinclair: Over all the years I've had clients, there was really only one that I'd prefer not to bring back on a hunting trip. There's no particular type that stands out as a kind I particularly dislike. You work to get to know a client, and sometimes it takes a little longer than other times before everybody gets comfortable. The challenge of being out there and getting the job done makes you work hard, whatever the client's attitude.

Dave Fyfe: I've dealt with hundreds of hunters, and literally thousands of fishermen, and I'll tell you what, I think most good guides and outfitters should be able to handle almost all the different personality types. Of course, some people are just outright rude or ignorant. But for the most part you can bring people around by the end of the hunt, because they're outdoors for recreation. I've found that even the sorts who are miserable back home usually come around to having a good time eventually.

The only ones I would refuse to guide are those who are just frankly unsafe to be around. By that I mean people who aren't familiar enough with firearm safety, or don't have enough respect for themselves or others to consider safety. If somebody points a loaded gun at me they lose all my respect, and I never take my eyes off a person like that. We've had two rifles discharged in camp accidentally, one while being loaded and another while being unloaded. It's very difficult to reestablish respect between guide and client when something like that happens. Safety has to be first, and everything else is a distant second. I really can't say I've ever had a hunter I wouldn't have back, though. I've had a couple of guys I wouldn't say I enjoyed being around, but I haven't yet met a client I wouldn't have back. I was a teacher before I became a guide and outfitter, but in this business I've learned more about people than I did while teaching.

Bill Perkins: I wouldn't hunt with someone who has to have the biggest and best bull no matter what. That is not the type of hunt I enjoy. Most guides do not enjoy that kind of hunter, and, if that's the way a person thinks, he can find someone else to guide him.

What is the worst thing a client can do on a hunt?

John Caid: In my book the worst thing is to show disrespect for the animal—for example, when an animal is wounded and the hunter's attitude is, "So what?" I'm out there working hard, trying to find the wounded animal, and he just doesn't seem to care.

Time for more glassing.

Hunters like that don't respect the animal, and part of the culture of the Tribes is respect for the animal. We keep that in mind at all times. Some clients, unfortunately, don't have that.

Allen Morris: The worst thing a hunter can do when I'm guiding is try to call the elk. They're paying me good money to be out there and be the guide and do the calling. Some hunters beg me to teach them, and they beg to call. As long as it's a teaching format and they understand that, it's fine. But when that bull's locked on and he's coming in to us, I don't want you to call. I don't want that bull even to know you're around. The worst thing a client can do is start calling when he's paying me to do the calling.

The other bad thing that's happened to me is when a client shoots two animals because he gets confused. Sometimes you've got two hundred elk in front of you, he shoots a bull, and the animal runs over the knob ahead. You run up and your hunter just cranks off another round, thinking it's the same bull. All of a sudden you've got two elk down, and you've got a nightmare. You call Fish and Game, he gets a fine, and things turn ugly. Situations like these always boil down to the hunter not following instructions.

Jack Atcheson Jr.: One thing I dislike is if the hunter fails to read the laws of the area he's hunting. A hunter like that never picks up a map or an area description that tells him what's legal and what isn't, and he puts all the burden on the guide. They've got to do their homework so they personally know what's legal. A guy might shoot a five-point elk in a six-point area and then blame the guide for not keeping him out of trouble. They've got to take some responsibility for their own actions.

Another thing is not being physically prepared, and that's becoming a bigger issue as the hunting population ages. You know, when I first started in this business, we never booked an elk hunt of less than fourteen days, but now the hunting trips are five to seven days and the hunters want bigger and bigger bulls. Underestimating the animal they're hunting is a big mistake, too.

Chad Schearer: I think the worst thing a client can do is to fail to give 110 percent effort. I had one fellow say to me, "I'm from down South. The deer there don't move when it's raining, so the elk won't move, either. I'm staying in camp today." Well, he made a big mistake, because everybody who went out got a shot at a bull that day. I think the worst thing a client can do is to be unwilling to give it his best effort.

Van Hale: The absolute worst thing a client can do is to be unsafe with a firearm. That's one thing we always worry about, even though it's never happened to us. There's no elk worth getting shot over. Guys get excited, and they can do some crazy things without thinking. A guy in another camp near here knocked down a bull a couple of years ago, and it fell down into a canyon. The guide and the outfitter both went down after it, and the hunter was looking through his scope at them down there. Somehow he touched the trigger, and he blew one guy's head off. That happened right here in our own back door.

Ross Johnson: When a hunter tries to run his own hunt, it's the worst thing he can do. We've taken out a lot of really good hunters over the years, really experienced people, and I can say that good, experienced hunters realize that each individual area has its own characteristics. They may know elk in Canada or Montana, but they might not understand them in the Southwest. The more experienced the client, the more he's willing to follow the guide's recommendations. The inexperienced hunter may read in a magazine that you're supposed to bugle or you're supposed to do this or that or the other, and then he may not listen to his guide, preferring to go his own way.

Ron Dube: Violating ethical practices, like being a game hog, is one of the worst things a client can do.

Rick Trusnovec: A hunter who violates firearms safety rules really sets me off. I've had guys point a loaded rifle at my back as we're going after a bull. If we're in close, I may have my client slip a shell into the chamber of his rifle. I have him hold the weapon across his chest and away from me, but sometimes they get tired of carrying it that way. Before you know it, he's carrying it in one hand and pointing it down at the ground; then it's aimed at my back or my head. When I catch a gun aimed at

Elk country.

me, I have to stop and tell the client to point that thing some other way. Having to do that ruins my concentration and takes my mind off that bull we're stalking.

Bob Fontana: I hate seeing people mishandle a firearm. It happens all the time, too, and it seems to be getting worse. I think it's because a lot of the hunters we're getting nowadays didn't grow up with a firearm in their hands and weren't taught safety by their father or grandfather out in the field. We actually spend a lot of time in our seminars going over firearms safety, because virtually all the time on our hunts the guide is walking in front of the hunter. I see so many hunters holding the barrel right up the guide's backside. It drives me crazy to see that. I think that's the worst thing.

Brent Sinclair: I think the worst thing is when the client won't make an honest effort to be successful. That is, he isn't willing to put in the effort that enables the guide to do his job.

Dave Fyfe: I can't stand it when a hunter has no respect for himself or the animals. I can handle most of the other things. I can handle a bit of a confrontation. I can handle someone questioning how we're doing things. I can also handle guys that maybe are a little bit miserable, because we can get them away from the rest of the people in camp. There are ways to handle most things. But for me personally, respect for safety and the animals are the two things that I consider sacred. A person who has no regard for safety, or who disrespects the animals we're hunting, he's the worst.

Bill Perkins: The worst thing a hunter can do is make misleading statements about his physical ability or his knowledge of the woods and his equipment.

How do you prepare for and handle "bull fever" in a hunter/client?

John Caid: When I feel a hunter is excitable, maybe because he's inexperienced, I put out a little extra effort. That's why we go through two to three days of just looking at bulls and telling him to relax. Sometimes we might practice pulling up on a bull, not pulling the trigger but just putting him in the sights, so as to try to get a guy over that problem during the first few days. After three or four days of going around and calmly looking at elk, we may see one of record book quality that we really like. I tell the hunter to get ready, this looks like a pretty good one, but I don't let myself get too excited about it.

If you display excitement to the hunter, obviously he's going to pick up on it, too. I calmly remind him of shot placement while he's getting ready, and when he's all set, I let him go ahead. Don't tell him it's the biggest elk you've ever seen, the way I did with my first hunter. He'll start puffing, no doubt, if you do. The first time I saw a really big bull, I got a little worked up and probably got my hunter too excited, because he missed it! One thing we can do as guides is to be calm for the hunter. I've accompanied a lot of guides with their clients, and sometimes I can see the guide's breathing speed up, I can hear his voice going up—he's just not calm. If the hunter senses that, he's going to pick up on it.

Allen Morris: You can't really prepare adequately for bull fever. I've had a lot of clients over the years call to ask me how they can get ready for their hunt. If they're archery hunters, I tell them to mentally visualize a bull elk running in close. If they're rifle hunting, I tell them to envision a bugling bull elk out there at 100 yards and that they've got to put those cross hairs on the shoulder and squeeze the trigger.

Jack Atcheson Jr.: Full-blown bull fever is a tough one. I try, as much as possible, not to have the hunter peeking over the ridge with me and viewing the animal for too long. If we're up on a ridgeline, I try to keep down the odds of the animal seeing us, so I ask the hunter to keep his head down. If we're bugling in an elk, a lot of times you don't see the animal until it's ten or fifteen yards away, and if your hunter is overly excited, it's tough. I avoid appearing overexcited myself, and that seems to help.

Chad Schearer: I don't know if a guy can ever be fully prepared for bull fever. The best cure I can see is to hunt more, because the more you're around these big animals, the more it helps you. One thing I tell hunters is not to look at the antlers. Once you've decided the animal is big enough, stop looking at the head and start picking your spot on the animal's body. If you have to, look away for a minute, catch your breath, and then take your shot. We do talk to the hunters ahead of time so they'll know what to expect. A good rest is probably the single most useful way of countering bull fever. I call those bipods guide insurance!

Van Hale: What we always do to counter disabling excitement is have a few meetings with the guides, in which we try to analyze each hunter. You just really have to talk to your hunter, tell him to calm down, not to focus on the antlers, and so on. There's no hard and fast rule. You're dealing with personalities and everybody's different, so all you can do is the best you can.

Ross Johnson: It's tough to handle overpowering excitement. I've watched other outfitters visiting from Alaska and elsewhere, or people who have hunted dangerous game in Africa, and when they see some of these 375+ bulls they just totally fall apart. It does different things at different times to different people. I had one major outfitter who hunted with us tell me, "If that bull hadn't bugled at me, I could have killed him!" So I think what we sell is adrenaline, and there's no real cure for it.

Ron Dube: Bull fever is something that we work on a lot. I think the best way to handle it is to become proficient with your firearm at the range before you go on your hunt. If you're confident that you can knock out a gnat's eye at a couple of hundred yards from a rest, that's going to help. And your guide can help. If he sees you breathing too hard, even though you haven't exerted yourself, that's bull fever, and we have to coach the client not to shoot until we can see that the muzzle isn't waving back and forth, and that his breathing is not labored. Only then do we allow him to take the shot. If that gun barrel is weaving, we pass the shot and say, "Don't shoot, don't shoot!" We don't even think about letting him shoot, in fact. I'll have people look through the scope and not have their finger in the trigger guard. When I feel confident that they can make the shot, I tell them to go ahead and squeeze carefully, to try to have the gun go off by surprise, without any jerking of the trigger.

Rick Trusnovec: When you've been in this business long enough, you can watch a client get his rifle out of the car at base camp and tell in the first five minutes how much he's handled his gun. That's often a good indicator of how susceptible he is to bull fever. When I'm in the field and I put a guy on a bull, I'm constantly watching him, how he's reacting. Has he got the shakes, has he all of a sudden almost started needing oxygen while you've been standing on a piece of flat ground for ten minutes? You've got to read the client beforehand in order to try to keep him calm.

What that means is to talk to him in a calm voice, tell him exactly what you want him to do, and do it in a relaxed manner. It's not good for me as the guide to get excited, which in turn excites the hunter even more. We may be looking at a heck of a bull, but if I think the hunter is excitable I really play it down. I quietly tell him where the bull is, get him a good rest, and tell him to relax. It's no big deal, it's not that big a bull anyway! No matter how big it is! I do this only with a guy who's inexperienced or overly excitable. I take a lot of trophy hunters, and usually I don't have to tell them anything like that. Even guys with a lot of experience can get excited, though, so you have to be able to read your hunter and try to keep things calm so he stays relaxed.

Bob Fontana: We talk about bull fever in the seminar. We're in a unique situation in that we put a lot of hunters in the middle of the rut for the first time. A lot of them have hunted elk before, but a lot of them have done those late-season hunts and so forth. We also have a lot of real first-timers, and they're certainly not prepared for all the excitement when you've got a bull squealing in your face and spitting on you and all that. We talk about it in the seminar, and then the guides and I really talk to them once we're in the field. We're pretty instructive, and in fact we're pretty demanding. We tell them everything that we think is going to happen and everything that we want them to do. We keep them very close to us. My favorite expression is "I want you right on my shoulder." We're very direct and specific, and we give instruction at a pretty good pace. We don't hold back anything, and especially because for five or six years we've had a six-point-only regulation in place. We have to be very instructive and be on top of those elk hunters at all times.

Brent Sinclair: If I get the chance, I have a little trick I do with inexperienced hunters to help them with bull fever. I like to simulate the real thing by telling the client to get ready in very serious fashion—as if we're really about to shoot something—just to see how he reacts. I tell him to take his time, to settle down, and not to rush. Being able to talk him through a starting-line situation before the fact can mean that he doesn't jerk the trigger ahead of the starting line when there's an elk in front of him. I use verbal communication to try to settle the client down and tell him to take his time and wait; there's no rush. It seems that approach is invaluable. I like to practice in this way a couple of times, if possible, before we even get on an elk, just so he's had a little experience and doesn't have to rush into the real thing.

Dave Fyfe: Handling bull fever gets back to the teaching thing, and the guide needs to be a little bit of a psychologist, being aware that it's a possibility in every hunter. Assessing the hunter—getting to know him ahead of time—helps a lot. I get a sense whether my hunter is going to get that excited or not. Generally guys with a lot of experience don't get out of control. If a person is fairly inexperienced or if he's never had an opportunity at a bull elk before, he's more susceptible. When it comes right down to it, I'm watching the hunter very, very carefully, and I do not let him shoot if he's too excited. I had one hunter miss a shot at eighty yards, and after his second shot I said, "Hand me your gun. We're going to look for another animal. But first we're going back to the range, because you're not shooting at this animal again." He was absolutely out of control, and he was even making noises before he pulled the trigger. So a big part of it is getting to know the hunter, then watching him very carefully and assessing his behavior, making sure he's calm enough to make the shot. I make it clear to them that generally you get only one chance because an elk doesn't often stick around to give the hunter a second one. It's important when you pull that trigger that the cross hairs are where you want them to be.

Bill Perkins: In the area we hunt, we have a rule of three points per side or better. I normally don't tell someone how big the bull is, just to hold down any nervousness. I tell him that it's legal and to get a good, comfortable spot from which to shoot. Then I tell him to relax, get comfortable breathing, and just squeeze the trigger.

Chapter 4

THE ELK GUIDES EVALUATE HUNTING ARMS

What is your favorite rifle caliber for elk?

John Caid: My personal favorite is the .300 Winchester Magnum. I like the gun and the way it shoots. The best all-round and the most popular is the .30-06. Back in the 1980s it seemed to be the .270 that everybody was bringing. In the last ten years the .300 Weatherby has been showing up a lot, and it's a great gun, too.

Allen Morris: Barring none, my favorite gun is the .338 Winchester Magnum. In all the guiding I've done for the last twenty years, the one caliber that has knocked elk off their feet and kept them on the ground is this one. The other caliber that I'm excited about, and we've had some clients bringing them in, is the Remington .300 Ultra Mag. It's knocking elk right off their feet, too. You shoot until they're down. I've seen some nightmares on maybe ten to fifteen hits, some of which didn't result in a kill because they knocked the bull down and it got up and ran off. They should have been putting in follow-up shots. With the .338 you usually don't need follow-ups.

Jack Atcheson Jr.: Any .30 caliber will do, though my all-time favorite is the .338 Winchester Magnum.

Chad Schearer: My favorite rifle caliber is the .338 Winchester Magnum.

Van Hale: A .300 Winchester or .300 Weatherby is my favorite. I like them because you don't have to shoot a really heavy-grain bullet. Our country is fairly open, so we shoot a long ways sometimes. These are very flat shooting, hard-hitting rifles. It seems that the hunters of today aren't the marksmen they were fifteen years ago. These guns will hit hard enough that even when the shot isn't perfect, you usually can catch up to the elk.

Ask the Elk Guides

Ross Johnson: Bigger is better. I don't have anything I'd really name. Anything from 7mm on up. The first governor's hunter we took used one of those big .300 or .338 things they're using nowadays, and I was absolutely amazed at how effective it was.

Ron Dube: I'd recommend the .338 Winchester Magnum. That's what I shoot.

Rick Trusnovec: I like the 7mm magnum. It's a pretty standard caliber that clients bring into my camps.

Bob Fontana: The .338 Winchester Magnum is without doubt my selection.

Brent Sinclair: The .338 Winchester Magnum is my personal favorite.

Dave Fyfe: I should tell you that I'm not really much of a technician, but I like the .300 Winchester Magnum.

Bill Perkins: My favorite all-round gun is a .338 that I had custom made. But I also carry a .30-378 for long-range hunting.

What caliber do you recommend for clients?

John Caid: I'd recommend they bring a gun they're comfortable shooting. I've always seen a problem when a guy books a hunt with us and then goes out and buys a huge caliber, something he's afraid to shoot. Maybe he's been at the range a few times with it, but he's not comfortable with it. I'd much rather see a hunter show up with a rifle, whether it's a .270 or a .300 or a .30-06, that he's shot a lot. Shot placement is far more critical than caliber. If they've been hunting with something like a .243, and they haven't bought a bigger rifle before, then personally I'd recommend a .30-06. A guy can still use it for deer, but with the 180-grain bullet it's great for elk, and he's got a good all-round gun. If he brings a really big gun and you see that he closes his eyes and turns his head when he shoots, you know it's going to be ugly.

Allen Morris: All other things being equal, I recommend the .338 Winchester Magnum.

Jack Atcheson Jr.: I have no quarrels with any .30 caliber, though my all-time favorite is the .338.

Chad Schearer: For my clients I recommend a minimum of a .270 caliber. I really try to stress a .30 caliber or larger. I've seen elk taken with everything from a .257 on up, but I want a guy to shoot as big a gun as he can without being afraid of the recoil. Sometimes guys will buy a really big caliber rifle, but they're afraid to shoot it; they shoot just awfully. I'd rather a hunter tone it down and buy a little smaller caliber so that he can drill the target every time at 100 yards. It doesn't matter how big your gun is if you can't put that shot where it needs to go.

Van Hale: For clients, I'd recommend the .300 Winchester or Weatherby, but if they've got a .270 they've been shooting all their life and they've killed twenty deer with it, then that's the gun I want them to bring. Basically, any caliber from .270 on up is good, if you're familiar with the gun and comfortable shooting it.

Ross Johnson: I've seen rifle hunters miss worse than archery hunters, so I want something big enough that if the elk is hit in a bad place we're still going to recover the animal.

Ron Dube: I recommend the .338 Winchester Magnum for my hunters, if they can shoot it, but I'd much rather they have a .270 if they can't shoot a .338. I want them to put the bullet where the elk lives!

Rick Trusnovec: The worst thing a client could do is go out and buy a big-caliber gun and be afraid to shoot it. A lot of guys go out and do that because they read that the minimum caliber for elk is a .338. The problem is that they can't shoot it. You've got to be comfortable with the gun you're shooting, whether it be a .30-06, a .300, a .270, or whatever—it really doesn't matter. Shot placement is what's important, and shot placement just isn't going to be there when you're shooting a big gun you're not comfortable with.

Bob Fontana: I personally prefer the .338, but for clients I recommend the .300 Winchester Magnum or better.

Brent Sinclair: I'd have to say that for a client I'd recommend a rifle that they shoot well. I've had hunters show up with a .300 Ultra Mag or a .375 Ultra Mag, and it's just way more than they can handle. They wound game or miss game, because they're scared of the rifle. I tell them to bring a weapon they feel comfortable shooting. It's all shot placement, and if you bring a brand-new magnum that you can't shoot, it can be a nightmare.

Dave Fyfe: I hunt with the .300 Winchester Magnum personally, and I recommend it for our clients.

Bill Perkins: Whatever they are comfortable shooting, starting with a .270 and up.

What is your advice on bullet weight? Bullet construction?

John Caid: I've had good luck, and seen good performance, with the Nosler Partition bullet. It's a really good bullet and seems to perform exactly as advertised. In the .30-06 we recommend 180 grains.

Allen Morris: My number one elk bullet, bar none, is the Trophy-Bonded Bearclaw by Speer. It is far and away the best bullet an elk hunter can put in his rifle. I recommend the 225-grain version, which is what I use in my .338. This bullet far outperforms the Nosler Partition. You're getting Al's opinion on all this, of course.

Jack Atcheson Jr.: I like heavy bullets. A lot of people think African animals are tough compared with North American animals; well, they haven't hunted elk. Elk are tough. Elk are famous for taking a hit, then getting up and walking away, never to be seen again. Shoot a heavy bullet, and shoot frequently. I like a partition bullet. You don't always get a perfect shot on an elk. I've noticed that more elk are hit closer to the tail than they are to the heart, so these bigger calibers can give you a little bit of an edge. When I hunt elk, I'll take them at any angle. I hunt elk in heavy timber, and I have to make pretty marginal shots sometimes. You shouldn't do that with a .270. I even have solids loaded up for my .338. Solids should often be used on animals that weigh over 500 pounds. Penetration is everything.

Chad Schearer: I like Nosler Partitions or Ballistic Tips. In the .338 I recommend the 225-grain bullet.

Van Hale: One of my new favorites is the Barnes X-Bullet, although the old Nosler Partition is hard to beat. As far as bullet weight, I think people tend to shoot too heavy a bullet in our country. It hinders more than it helps. My favorite bullet weight, and I'm probably going against the grain here, is 150 to 165 grains, never to exceed 180 grains. If we hunted thicker country, I'd have a different opinion. Here a 300-yard shot is not uncommon, and a 225-grain bullet drops like a rock after 200 yards.

Ross Johnson: I tend to lean more to the flatter-shooting, lighter-weight bullets, such as the Nosler Partition and the Barnes X-Bullet, which hold their weight well.

Ron Dube: I don't think the bullet is critical, unless it's a little caliber. With a .270 you're going to have to use 150-grain bullets; a 7mm you're going to be up at 160 to 165 grains. In a .338 it should be 200 to 225 grains. The bigger the bullet the better.

Rick Trusnovec: I don't have a favorite bullet. There are so many out there that do the job properly these days. Ballistics and bullets are so darned good today that it really doesn't matter.

Bob Fontana: I like the heavy bullets. I'm a big-bore fan. If someone asked me whether to bring a .30-06 or .375 H&H, I'd tell him the .375. And use the heaviest bullets the rifle shoots well. I like the Trophy Bonded Bear Claw and the Swift A-Frame. I also like the Winchester Fail-Safe, though it might produce a little too much penetration on a herd animal like elk, so you could wind up with more elk than you have tags for. Those are three of my favorites.

Brent Sinclair: I like a heavy-construction bullet: in the .338 a 225- or 250-grain bullet. I like the Barnes type, or Bear Claw—something that maintains a good weight retention so you get the maximum performance. I also like the Nosler Partition bullets, which generally don't come apart. Barnes has a tremendous design with claws that come out without losing much bullet mass. I see a lot of elk needing a second shot just because of a lightweight bullet construction that lets the bullet come apart. I like the good old H-frame or A-frame bullets.

Dave Fyfe: I use and recommend the 165- or 180-grain Speer Grand Slam.

A few bulls to evaluate.

Bill Perkins: For elk I believe 160 grains and above is preferred. I use 180- to 210-grain Barnes or Nosler bullets.

Do you have any tips on shooting techniques in field situations?

John Caid: You know, our shots are relatively close. We try to have them sighted out to 300 yards, but we know where it's going to hit at 200 and 100 yards, and even closer. You're not always going to be in a shooting position, or standing there beside a rest. Sometimes you can't get a rest. Practice often, and practice at lots of different angles—practice kneeling, practice standing, both with and without a rest, and practice in a lot of different situations. Shoot a little uphill and downhill, because you're not always on a flat. Most people go to the range and shoot a few times to make sure their gun is on, but they don't really practice for the odd situation, where you're shooting up or down off the side of a hill. A lot of times in those situations they'll shoot right over the top of the animal.

Allen Morris: As for shooting, when we go out and sight in, I teach people to wrap that sling around their elbow. I've taught a lot of guys how to do that, how to get a good tight configuration, and it really seems to help. Also, I don't like to let people shoot over 100 yards at elk. Last year was the first year (I can brag) that we took sixty-five rifle hunters and did not have one single wounding loss. That was the first year in twelve years of professional guiding that I didn't lose an elk on a rifle hunt.

Jack Atcheson Jr.: Getting a good rest is number one when it comes to shooting. Shooting offhand is last-ditch unless you're really close. Guiding a lot of hunters, I always had a couple of bipods in camp, even though a bipod adds weight to a hunter's gun. We found that the odds of a hunter getting onto that good trophy animal and making a killing shot were so much higher using the bipod than leaning over a backpack or up against a tree. A bipod is one of the single biggest improvements you can make. If you miss that bull elk, you might not get another chance, or your next chance might be a four-point or something instead of a big bull. The first shot is so important, too, since elk aren't known for standing around and begging for a second bullet. They're usually running like crazy after the first shot.

Chad Schearer: One thing I recommend is that a guy get his breath before shooting. If you know where the elk are located and you've been huffing it and hoofing it to get to the top of the mountain, stop and take a minute to catch your breath before you shoot. The other thing I recommend is to have a pair of Crooked Horn Outfitters' shooting sticks, or else a Harris bipod. A lot of times bipods are used when hunting mule deer and antelope, but I also recommend them for elk hunters.

Van Hale: In today's hunting industry, where so many of our clients come from the East and they're not used to shooting long range, I think the best advice I could give is to bring a pair of shooting sticks. There are very few guys anymore who can just throw up the rifle freehand at two hundred yards and knock something down. Some of the shooting sticks are really compact, they fit nicely in your backpack, and they're certainly handy to have. Getting a good rest is going to make a difference in whether you take an animal home or not. Bipods are okay, but usually the grass is too high, and the bipod won't fit in a saddle scabbard.

Ross Johnson: The best advice I can offer on shooting is to stay calm. That's one of the main things our guides try to get our hunters to do. We hunt an awful lot of really big elk, and we want to get the hunter's mind off the elk. We try to get the hunter to pick a spot on the elk, like a muddy spot on the side of the animal, and the guide will bet him a hundred bucks he can't hit that spot. What's important is to get the hunter's mind off the elk and onto something else.

Ron Dube: One solid recommendation is to always, always, always use a rest. In case that's not possible, you must be proficient with your firearm for offhand shots at reasonable ranges. I believe anybody ought to be able to hit an elk in the chest offhand with a scoped rifle when it's standing broadside at 100 yards. If you can't do that because of "bull fever," or not being proficient with a firearm, you shouldn't be hunting in the first place. We're trying to kill these animals, not hurt them!

Rick Trusnovec: My advice for shooting is to always get a rest. There may be a few times when you walk up on game, they see you the same moment you see them, and you've got the shot and you've got to take it. But in most situations, I'll never let a guy take a shot without a rest.

Bob Fontana: I think I read it first in one of Carmichael's books, but, as to shooting, I like hunters who can get in a good, solid rest position quickly. Not very many are good at it. I like sitting with a sling wrap, which is probably one of the better field positions, or when a guy can quickly set up against a jack pine or an aspen tree. I like hunters that are thinking ahead, thinking about where they're going to get that good, solid rest— especially if you're in a bugling encounter or you've got something going on right in front of you.

Brent Sinclair: I carry a little two-foot piece of string that I loop over my knees to stabilize them. I also use it a lot for glassing. I just tie the rope on my belt, and when I need it I flip it over my knees and pull it tight. If there's no tree or rock to lean on, you can sit down, pull the string tight, put your elbows on your knees, and shoot from right there. The stability is like a rock. It's an old sheep hunter trick I learned from Bert Regal back in the 1970s, and I've used it ever since. I use it more for glassing than for shooting, but it works great either way. Every situation in the field is different, so just get the best rest you can and make the best shot you can.

Dave Fyfe: Whenever I'm guiding and we're in the field, I never stop to glass or look over an area without situating my hunter so he's in a position to make the shot if I spot the animal. I remember so many times making the sighting and having

A big Rocky Mountain bull easing through the timber.

nowhere to set up to make the shot, and by the time you get ready the animal's gone. The one thing I do consciously now is to always look for a place where the hunter can set up immediately if I spot an animal.

Bill Perkins: Shooting in the coastal ranges of Oregon or Washington can easily vary between fifty and two hundred yards, and it's mostly freehand. So know what you are able to do, freehand, kneeling, and using different types of rests, such as a walking stick, a limb, or a stump. The main thing with all types of hunting is to know what you are able to do with your equipment. Don't take shots that you don't feel comfortable taking. You might lose the bull. Try to get within your comfort range so you know that you can make a good hit on the animal and thereby have less chance of losing it. I have found a number of animals in the woods dead from bad shots, or made by people who didn't know how to track a wounded animal. That is a great loss to everyone when it happens. Know your ability!

Do you have any wise words on bowhunting? Black powder hunting?

John Caid: We haven't had a great many black powder hunters on the White Mountain Apache Reservation, so I don't know a great deal about it. We do have a lot of bowhunters, though. They always seem to need a challenge. We have some bowhunters come in because it's easier to get a record book bull with a bow. I think they should bow hunt for the right reasons—because they enjoy the challenge. A lot of them are very good hunters. We've had some celebrities that are absolutely outstanding and very serious about their hunting. Because bowhunters are generally very good hunters, I don't have a lot of advice for them. We've had a few woundings from people who wanted to be bowhunters, but the majority are excellent. I don't try to tell them what to do.

Allen Morris: Bowhunters tend to hide behind things, and in an elk hunting situation you need to be well camouflaged and in front of the tree or bush to get the opportunity to harvest that elk. So many guys like to bury themselves in holes—it's that they've hunted whitetails their whole life. But with elk you need to get in front of those obstructions so you can get a clear shot. Black powder hunters, they say, do it because bowhunting is too difficult and rifle hunting is too easy. Black powder was tailor-made for elk hunting. You can get most bulls within fifty to eighty yards. Getting that next thirty to forty yards is real tough, but getting within one hundred yards is fairly easy.

Jack Atcheson Jr.: Bowhunting elk is definitely a graduate level hunting trip. A lot of people think, okay, I'm going to go out on a bow hunt for my first elk hunt. That's the reverse of how it ought to be. You ought to go on a rifle hunt first, then do a bow hunt. The best advice I could give an archery hunter is to get an elk or two under his belt with a rifle before going archery hunting. There will be a lot more happy endings. Black powder hunting is the same. You've really got to be familiar with your weapon, and be practiced on reloading a second shot. Try to make a muzzleloader or archery hunt something that comes later, rather than being your first elk hunting experience.

Chad Schearer: I guide for both bowhunting and black powder. It's when bowhunting that you're going to use most of your calling techniques. I really like to use the Knight-Hale diaphragm elk calls, because you can be hands-free in your calling. You can get full draw on your bull when he's coming in, and still give him a cow call to stop him.

Another thing is to just tune your bow. I am a really strong advocate of using fixed-blade broadheads on these big bull elk. And use a broadhead that's heavy enough. I shoot a 125-grain Satellite broadhead, because I like something with a lot of kinetic energy.

You should practice your shots in hunting conditions, not at 20- or 30-yard range conditions. You may be shooting down over rocks or through limbs. Put your targets in the woods to practice. And try running ten to twenty yards or so, then pulling your arrow out and shooting, so you've got that adrenaline factor going and your heart pumping.

Ask the Elk Guides

As for black powder, I'm guest host of the *Black Powder Guns and Hunting* television show, which will be coming up on the Outdoor Life Network. I use the Winchester Apex 209 in .50 caliber. However, with today's new bullets I'm using the .45 caliber on a lot of my elk hunts, because I get a lot better velocity out of it. With the Powerbelt bullets you can get more distance, it's easier loading, and you can take elk at 200 yards—it really does the job. The big thing with black powder is to make sure you try different loads. With the magnum loads, I use 150 grains of Pyrodex pellets and the 275-grain bullet. You should be sure to foul the barrel after you clean it so it remains accurate. I recommend putting in both the powder and the bullet. Some guys just put in a couple of Pyrodex pellets and shoot it, but you don't have an equal pressure all the way down the barrel, and it doesn't foul properly. A clean barrel on a muzzleloader will shoot much differently from a dirty barrel (as much as four to six inches). So the sequence is to clean it well, and then foul it so it shoots accurately. The final thing is to make sure you know the local regulations, because many places have special rules that apply only to black powder firearms.

Van Hale: We do a lot of both black powder and archery hunting. The archer owes it to the animal to be proficient with his weapon. That also goes, by the way, for the black powder hunter, because a lot more proficiency is required than when hunting with a modern rifle. That fact is generally overlooked today, and a lot of guys will buy a muzzleloader and shoot it a half-dozen times before they come. If they hit the paper they think that's good, but it's not nearly enough. It's the same thing with the bow. You need to practice to be good at it.

Ross Johnson: We take forty to fifty bowhunters a year, and again, what's important is to pick a spot, relax, and try to forget the animal you're shooting at. Concentrate on that spot. For both archery and black powder, it comes down to knowing your capabilities. That's where our questionnaire comes in; we hand that information to the guides. They will know if their hunter is comfortable shooting a muzzleloader at 100 yards or 150 yards or whatever. It's the hunter's responsibility to put down the range at which he feels comfortable, and it's the guide's problem to get him within that range.

Ron Dube: Bowhunting is tough. If a guy has lots of experience, and he's killed a lot of game, it's much easier for him. I tell people that if they've never killed a deer before they're probably going to have a hard time killing an elk with a bow because of the excitement. Probably the most important factor in being a successful bowhunter on a guided elk hunt is to have put in a lot of practice and to be confident in your ability to place the arrow where it needs to go. That comes from practice, practice, and more practice. Some people require more practice than others. Some people are calmer than others. Black powder is just like rifle hunting, really, especially with the modern black powder firearms. And the average guy who's a gung-ho black powder fanatic is usually a pretty good shot and knows his limitations.

Rick Trusnovec: Black powder, no. As for bowhunting, so many people go overboard about concealment. So many guys set up behind trees or behind brush, but they need to be out front so they have a clear shot. If that bull comes in, you don't move a muscle; the bull is concentrating on me, not the hunter. I always keep in steady eye contact with the hunter, because there are too many times when the guy behind sees a bull trying to circle and the hunter doesn't. Staying in eye contact is everything, so that everybody knows what's going on.

Bob Fontana: We take bowhunters because here in southern British Columbia we have an exclusive bow season that starts on the first of September and goes to the tenth. I enjoy it, though it's still not my favorite way to harvest an elk. A word to the wise for bowhunters is to practice, practice, practice. We've had some bulls wounded and lost with archery tackle. We have very few black powder hunters.

Brent Sinclair: My top suggestion on archery would be to make certain you have sharp broadheads. People often don't take that extra little time to be sure their broadheads are sharp. A lot of fellows like to shoot broadheads out of their bow so they'll know exactly how they fly, but you've got to sharpen them again afterward. Sharp broadheads are as important to the archery hunter as selecting the proper caliber of rifle for elk. For black powder, the trick is just having a round ball or bullet that has enough weight retention to do the job. Soft lead projectiles really don't do a good job.

Dave Fyfe: I don't have a lot of experience on either. Last year Jim Shockey hunted with us, however, and he did take the number one Roosevelt bull taken with black powder.

Bill Perkins: I've very little experience with either black powder or archery hunting.

Chapter 5

HUNTING ELK WITH THE GUIDES

What constitutes a successful hunt, from your perspective?

John Caid: A client that's happy and wants to return, whether he's gotten a big bull, an average bull, or just had a great hunt and didn't take a bull. We've had a lot of hunters that have hunted the full seven days, never pulled the trigger, and were so happy they were ready to book for next year. So to me it's a client who's happy with what we've done.

Allen Morris: A successful hunt means meeting the expectations of the client, but unfortunately too many people measure success based on the kill. If a successful hunt for someone is to come out and spend time with good people, eat good food, and walk in these Rocky Mountains watching bull elk in September, then that's a successful hunt. All the preparation, mental and physical, getting equipment ready, then going out and having a good time watching the natural world—that's what constitutes a successful hunt to me.

Jack Atcheson Jr.: As a booking agent, my perspective varies from region to region. If you take a wilderness area hunt in Idaho, Montana, or British Columbia, and the outfitter can maintain a 50 percent or better ratio on branch-antlered bulls, that man is running a really good show. And if maybe 30 percent of the bulls are six-pointers, if you're going to measure it by dead animals, that's successful. To me, though, a successful elk hunt is going out and hunting hard the whole time, seeing some elk, making some stalks, and enjoying the experience. Killing an elk isn't the whole picture. Harvesting an animal is nothing unless there is a hunt involved.

Chad Schearer: A happy client is my measure of success. I've had some successful hunts in which we haven't harvested an elk, but the client was outrageously happy just to be out there and experiencing it. Especially with bowhunting, you might get a huge bull to come in, but you don't get the shot; he's out there screaming at twenty yards yet doesn't give you an opportunity. I have a saying I attribute to George E. Mann of Alabama: "The essence of the hunt is of far greater importance than the result of the hunt." Everything that goes into the hunt is what makes the hunt. Pulling the trigger takes one second and it's over. A successful hunt is getting out there and having a good time with people you enjoy.

Van Hale: Of course everyone tends to say that a kill makes a successful hunt. In my opinion a successful hunt is when both the guide and client had a good time, and they saw and had opportunity to take animals in the field, even if they didn't kill an elk. If the client is happy and had a great time, and he wants to come back, that's certainly a successful hunt.

Ross Johnson: A hunter who's seen game, he got into elk, he's heard elk bugling, he's seen elk, he's had a good time—that's a successful hunt. It's camaraderie in camp, a slap on the back over a really good stalk, that kind of stuff. I don't think the kill is that important. The kill is the result, but I don't think it's what makes a good hunt.

Ron Dube: Well, obviously, everybody who comes out hopes to kill an elk. Whether you kill one or not, in my opinion, is not as important as the quality of the total wilderness experience, which results from having a positive attitude. The big majority of my clients who come on our truly rigorous wilderness elk hunts are looking for the total package. Those are the kinds of people that we market to, and I tell people that if they've never killed an elk before, shoot the first nice one you see. You can always come back later and look for a bigger one. If you have your heart set on a big one, though, be prepared to go home without one—and maintain that positive attitude. The big majority of our clients who don't get their animal—and that's not very many, because our success rate is very high—are not upset about it. They know we don't run a game farm, but our success rate is as high as anywhere in the country for wilderness elk hunts.

Rick Trusnovec: A successful hunt from my perspective as a business owner is keeping proper management over that business, keeping good employees, keeping good stock, keeping quality gear in camp, and keeping my hunters fed as well as they eat at home. If we happen to see and get close to elk, and even harvest a few, so much the better. We run a business where there's an owner in each camp. All my clients deal with an owner in camp, and that keeps proper management across the board with my clients, my camps, my employees, and all. I know if my clients are having a good time, and whether they're upset about anything. You can fix a lot of problems right there in camp without having to wait until it's all over. That keeps our success high, from our perspective.

Bob Fontana: Success is being in good country where you know there are lots of elk, enjoying that good-looking elk country, and enjoying the company of your guide. Of course you need to have the presence of elk, and we do because we hunt them during the rut. We hear them, smell them, and find wallows and rub trees, sign, and a lot of activity. Of course having opportunities to harvest an elk is important, but just knowing you're close to elk and enjoying it constitutes a successful hunt. I'm not here to tell you that we're selling a glorified pack trip, and I do think the kill is a big part of it, but I think being in among the elk is a bigger part.

Brent Sinclair: To me success is knowing that you've given an honest effort to provide the client with an opportunity, doing all you can do that is legal and ethical and complies with game laws. It's doing everything that you can to ensure that he has a good hunt, whether he harvests an animal or not. I've had clients who have had really bad experiences with other guides, even though they took a great animal. I've had some fellows who have hunted with the best guides in the country without harvesting an animal, but they had a great experience because the person they were with gave 110 percent effort.

Dave Fyfe: I'd consider a hunt successful if it were tailored to the individual hunter's goals and resulted in a satisfied hunter. We're very fortunate in that everybody who comes with us will take an elk. We did have one guy who didn't shoot a bull, but he had a goal of top-ten Boone and Crockett. That's a lofty goal, and I respected him for it. He was happy when he left. But twenty-six of our twenty-seven hunters have taken B&C bulls, so we're in an enviable position.

Ask the Elk Guides

Bill Perkins: I believe that a successful hunt is judged by what you learned, not necessarily by the animal you harvested. Hosting good friends and building new friendships is why I enjoy doing it.

What is the most common mistake made by guided hunters?

John Caid: I'd say the most common mistake is not listening to their guide. It may be their third or fourth elk hunt, and they come to the White Mountain Apache Reservation thinking they know big

Is there an elk out there somewhere?

elk. In that case they shoot a little bit too quickly if they don't listen when their guide tells them to hold up and wait.

Allen Morris: You know, I think most guys, if they haven't been out West before, don't understand the footwork involved on an elk hunt, and a lot of them don't pay attention to little things. They buy a new pair of boots and don't wear them before they get out here, and then they blister up their feet right away. That's one of the most common mistakes I see. People who have been on guided hunts know that their feet are required equipment, and they take better care of themselves and get those boots broken in before they get here.

Jack Atcheson Jr.: A very common mistake is turning down a bull that you shouldn't. A lot of folks will buy a hunt that's a two-hunter, one guide deal, which should never be considered a trophy elk hunt. A lot of hunters try to work a bargain elk hunt, and that reduces their chances by 50 percent right off the bat, because there aren't that many old bulls out there.

Chad Schearer: Not being prepared for the hunt is a common mistake. Also, not doing enough shooting practice. Another thing is buying brand new equipment and not breaking it in, something that's especially true of boots. When I see guys take out boots that are brand new, I know they're going to have a problem with blisters. I see that an awful lot. Some of these hunts can really involve a lot of walking. We walked fifty miles in five days down in New Mexico just this year on a hunt. You need to have good equipment, to be prepared, and to know what your equipment will do. Guys will sometimes spend $4,000 on an elk hunt and bring a rusty old rifle that can't shoot straight, or that has a scope with something wrong with it. I'd rather a guy save his money and get some good equipment so he can come later, rather than to show up with bad equipment that won't do the job.

Van Hale: A common mistake is misjudging the distance to the animal you're shooting at. Sometimes hunters won't listen to their guide when he tells them that a bull is three hundred yards away, because they think it's farther or not as far. Maybe they come from the East, where they don't shoot that far. The hunter and guide have to be on the same page. If the hunter has confidence in his guide, he's much more likely to listen to him.

Ask the Elk Guides

Ross Johnson: The most common mistake? They're never ready. Archery hunters, muzzleloader hunters, all of them—they're never ready to take the shot. They're always waiting for a picture-perfect situation, and they're never ready when the best opportunity they're going to get presents itself. It happens all the time.

Ron Dube: As far as shooting is concerned, the most common error is probably aiming too high, believing that the game is farther away than it really is, and overshooting. Another mistake is not getting into reasonable physical condition, not preparing enough to do what's necessary. If a guy puts forth the necessary effort, a guide sure appreciates that. Also, many people bring too much gear for a horseback hunt. It has no real effect on whether or not they kill an elk, but it's a problem for the outfitter.

Rick Trusnovec: So many guys come in with variable scopes on their rifles. A lot of times I happen to peek at their rifle when we start hunting, and they're cranked all the way up to nine or twelve power. That doesn't make sense. That power is obviously available for the three hundred yard shot when your game doesn't know you're there. You need to be prepared for what you might walk up on. That means having your scope turned down to its lowest power. To me it's a no brainer, but you'd be surprised how many guys make that mistake.

Bob Fontana: Not listening is one very common mistake. I guess where it breaks down is at the moment of truth, losing focus at the most critical time. It's that bull fever thing. They have this slack-jawed reaction and can't put anything together.

Brent Sinclair: One of the common mistakes hunters make is not listening, not paying attention, and instead, second-guessing the guide. Getting second-guessed by a client can be a big problem. You tell somebody to do something, and they decide, "Well, I'll go over here instead of staying put, because I think it's better." It can create real problems and lost opportunities when the client doesn't trust the guide to do what you've hired him to do.

Dave Fyfe: This question takes us back to mental preparation. I'd say that having unrealistic expectations of the hunt, the area, the weather, and so forth are common mistakes. A hunter sets himself up for disappointment if he has unrealistic expectations.

Bill Perkins: Not listening is a serious problem. If you picked your guide wisely, don't try to tell him how to do his job. Listen to him first, and then ask questions. If you feel you have a better idea, a good guide will listen if you come across as someone with knowledge. Trust me, he will know if you have a good head on you after only a short time in the woods. Guides can always learn something new and should be open to it. But as a hunter/client don't come across as if you're sure your way is the only way.

What can a guided hunter do that would most improve his chances of taking game?

John Caid: Physical fitness is number one. You increase your chances a whole lot if you can get around. Some of these big, old bulls live down in some of the deepest, thickest bottoms they can reach. Being able to get there definitely improves your chances, because you see more elk by just being able to move. Next is shot placement when the time comes. Being able to put the bullet where you need to is so important.

Allen Morris: I think mental preparation needs to be first on the list when it comes to improving your chances of taking game. And patience certainly plays a role when you're actually out there hunting elk. Hunters certainly need to practice with their gun or bow and know they can hit consistently and have confidence at one hundred yards with a rifle or thirty yards with a bow. Then they need to put themselves mentally in those situations before they get here.

Jack Atcheson Jr.: Mental preparation would top my list when it comes to improving your chances. I'd also recommend asking some point-blank questions of the outfitter about how many bulls are in the area. You should call some neutral game manager from the game department; they might tell you that in the area where you're thinking about going they have a 15 percent success ratio on any size bull elk. That's going to say a lot. They might tell you that the average hunter hunts six days to kill a three-point bull. Learn how to score elk. If you want a 350 bull, learn how to judge elk. A lot of guides don't measure elk for the hunter; they just show them to you and say, "That's a good one." And you've got to practice with the weapon, of course.

This packtrain is going elk hunting.

Chad Schearer: The most important single thing you can do is to listen to your guide. Don't pass up a bull on the first day if you'd be happy with that bull on the last day. Sometimes you're up there the first morning, the sun is coming up, and there's a real nice five- or six-point bull standing there. You tell yourself that it's a nice bull, but this is the first morning and you don't want your hunt to end. You may think that since you're seeing this bull, you will see lots of them. Sometimes elk hunting is fickle, and that might be the only bull, or the only decent bull, you see all week. To improve your chances, I recommend that you not pass up a bull you'd be happy with. The other thing is to practice shooting your weapon. Take your ballistics chart—you can download it off the Internet or get it from a book. Personally, I prefer to make an individual one for my own gun by shooting at different distances. Get a little white piece of paper and put on it what your gun will do if it's sighted in at, say, an inch and a half high at one hundred; where is it at two hundred and three hundred? Write that down and keep it with you. The last thing is that if you've got a shot into an elk, put another shot in him just to be sure he doesn't get up and take off.

Van Hale: Physical fitness is one of the biggest things you can do to improve your chances of success. If you can't get to where the animals are, you obviously aren't going to kill one. That's a big problem for us.

Ross Johnson: Practice with the weapon, physical conditioning, and mental preparation all improve your chances. Then just go read *Playboy* and forget the rest of it.

Ron Dube: The most important factor in improving your chances is to practice with your weapon and get good with it. Also, get into the best physical condition you can. Do a little horseback riding before you come. Try to cultivate a positive attitude.

Rick Trusnovec: Physical fitness is right at the top. Practicing with the weapon of choice is right at the top, too. I couldn't tell you how many guys have spent thousands of dollars on a trip with us, and they had either hardly shot or never shot their gun. I don't understand that. It just amazes me. They're not really prepared to hunt the game they're coming out to hunt. They haven't shot their firearm, they don't know if it's sighted in, and it happens so often. Mental preparation is also important, and just being willing to listen to your guide. You're paying us for our expertise. Why not use it?

Bob Fontana: Mental preparation, being able to maintain focus at the critical time, is so important to success. Physical fitness is likewise important because of where we hunt. It's pretty tough terrain, and sometimes you've got to get after those elk when they're bugling. Practice with the weapon is a big one, and almost nobody does it. Eighty percent of the clients that come up here have had their gun scoped and sighted by their gunsmith, and have taken maybe two shots off the bench themselves. They show up in camp and haven't done nearly enough shooting. They need to practice shooting from field positions—prone, kneeling, and so on. I don't know how I would rank them, but attention to all these factors improves a hunter's chances dramatically.

Ask the Elk Guides

Brent Sinclair: Physical conditioning definitely improves your chance of success. You get up into elk country, and it's not all three thousand feet elevation—some of it is seven or eight thousand. Lack of physical conditioning seems to be the biggest hindrance, in that some hunters just can't go where they need to go.

Dave Fyfe: Mental preparation comes first, and close behind is patience. The hunter's mental state is critical to a successful hunt.

Bill Perkins: Hunting Roosevelt elk on the coast range takes more than the normal complement of patience. I know people who have gone fifteen to twenty years without getting a bull. Even if you do all the right things, it could take up to three years to get that first bull; or if you're lucky it could happen the first year.

Besides the weapon, what kind of equipment should every hunter carry? Again besides the weapon, what is the most important single piece of equipment?

John Caid: Everyone should have a binocular, but boots can turn out to be the most important. You need a binocular while you're hunting in order to be able to look at these animals and enjoy them. We're going to describe the elk and talk about them while we're hunting, and hunters really need a good binocular. Make sure the boots are broken in so you don't get blisters. We do a lot of walking on both the White Mountain and the Havasupai Reservations, and blistered feet will slow you down more than anything. It's a huge thing to keep your feet comfortable for those seven days, because you'll put on a lot of miles.

Allen Morris: As for equipment, I think optics, having a really good binocular, is extremely important. For years I owned a cheap $79 binocular. For the first three or four years I guided, I thought that was all a man needed. Then I did a show with Wayne Pearson on Outdoors USA, and Zeiss wanted us to use its binoculars. They sent us a couple of binoculars as demos. I put those fine optics on my neck, and it has changed the way I hunt. I hunt much more efficiently now. I can see more, and I don't think guys understand how critical their eyes can be, even when they're hunting heavily timbered places, where they don't

Rocky Mountain elk grazing near heavy timber.

think optics will help. When you're sneaking through heavy pines, stop and glass down sixty or one hundred yards. You'll be amazed at what truly fine optics will reveal.

Jack Atcheson Jr.: Your boots and your binocular are a toss-up in my mind. Good boots are really important. Blistered feet won't do too much moving around. A good binocular and knowing how to use it will almost certainly influence whether or not you find elk. Don't just rely on the guide—get in there and do your part. That's true whether you're hunting in open country or in heavy timber. When I can't see very far ahead I take ten or twenty steps and I glass, looking for hair or an eyeball or anything that will help me get an edge on that elk.

Chad Schearer: I'd say the most essential piece of gear is good-quality optics. Besides having a good weapon, put a high-quality scope on your rifle. Some guys will buy an eight hundred dollar rifle and put a forty-nine dollar scope on it. I recommend a good scope. I also recommend having a good binocular, because we spend a lot of time out there glassing for elk. They should also have good boots, good clothing, as well as a really good daypack. One of the most important pieces of equipment is a cow call, regardless of whether you're a bowhunter, a muzzleloader hunter, or a rifle hunter. A lot of times when you have a bull moving away from you or moving through the timber, you blow that cow call and it stops him so you can get a shot. I also blow my cow call when I'm walking through the woods, because if I make any noise, such as stepping on a twig, it sounds like another elk walking. Then I have a better chance of getting close to a bedded bull.

Van Hale: My top recommended equipment would be a good binocular.

Ross Johnson: My suggestion on necessary equipment is a little unconventional, but I think it's important to have a GPS or cell phone, in case there's a problem in the field like a heart attack. We're very safety-conscious, and we stress CPR and first aid, but the hunter should carry some first aid items along, too.

Ron Dube: Binoculars are a vital item. Many hunters bring not only binoculars but also spotting scopes, rangefinders, and the like. I discourage them from bringing all that stuff if they're not willing to carry it on their person while they're hunting. My saddle horses are not packhorses, and there's no reason for a guy to carry all that extra gear if he's not going to use it. I do get clients from time to time who don't even bring flashlights or knives because they confer all the responsibility for their health and safety onto the guide. I've even had international hunters who have killed all kinds of exotic stuff, but when it got dark I've had to lend them a flashlight! They'd say, why do I need one? The guide has one. Clients should participate by actively looking for game with their own binoculars. If they're physically capable of carrying the rangefinder and spotting scope, fine—that way they don't have to take turns with the guide looking at the animal. But if they aren't comfortable carrying those personally, that's where the guide comes in. I always have a rangefinder and spotting scope with me at all times.

Rick Trusnovec: A good, quiet daypack and quiet clothing are tops in my estimation, when it comes to equipment.

Bob Fontana: A binocular is the most essential item of equipment, for a couple of reasons. A hunter might not be very helpful in glassing, but glassing for themselves makes them a part of the hunt. It allows them to enjoy their hunt more. If they come here and sit on their horse, or get off the horse and stand around waiting for the guide to find something for them to shoot, and maintain that type of attitude, then they're not hunters, they're shooters; they can't possibly enjoy the trip nearly as much. They're just not part of the hunt if they aren't glassing and looking themselves.

Brent Sinclair: For the guide, the most important gear is optics. If you can't glass them, you can't find them. For the hunter, it's clothing and footwear. I've seen many clients who were uncomfortable from being wet and cold, and we have had to return to camp early or leave an area and move around because they did not have the clothing to withstand the conditions thrown at them by the forces of nature. Footwear is as important as your rifle, because blistered feet will never get a hunter into those remote areas where big bulls like to live. Some parts of elk country are not accessible by horseback and require footwork to get to where the elk are. Clients pay top dollar for a guide/outfitter to get them an opportunity to harvest an elk, and if you do not have the right clothing and footwear, it's difficult for the guide to do his part.

Dave Fyfe: Good optics are absolutely essential. When I go hunting, if I forget my rifle, I may still go hunting just to get out in the woods. If I forget my binocular, I turn around and go home. I will not be out in the woods without my binocular.

Bill Perkins: In the coastal rain forest a good compass or GPS is highly recommended. If you are not familiar with the area you can get turned around very easily. I'd also highly recommend a good relief map of the area. And don't try learning skills with these items after you get lost in the woods. Make sure you know how to use them before going into the wilderness. A good binocular, a knife with a good edge, a small saw, and good rain gear are essential for hunting the Pacific Northwest.

Ask the Elk Guides

Are there any common items of equipment that you feel are unnecessary, redundant, or just plain worthless for hunting elk?

John Caid: You can carry only so much stuff out there. For the most part you don't need rangefinders and spotting scopes for elk hunting with us, because we're in close. They're not worthless, but they may not be worth carrying.

Allen Morris: You know, a lot of guys get caught up with having bipods, shooting sticks, and the like. I won't go hunt coyotes without my sticks, because I'm a better coyote hunter with them. But when you're hunting elk with us there's almost always a tree to grab, or something to rest on if you need it. I think a lot of guys have missed opportunities because they were more worried about getting their bipods down. Most of my elk shots are 100 yards or less. Most guys can even freehand at 100 yards if they have to. If you spend time worrying about the bipod, if that's your crutch, then you're going to miss opportunities. Some guys will tell you they're more successful because of it, but I don't think an elk hunter really needs a bipod or a set of sticks. You spend more time messing with it than you need to. So I frown on them for hunting elk, and I think they've been oversold.

Jack Atcheson Jr.: Too much equipment in general is the problem. Most people bring way too much of everything. In the situations I've guided, I do think a spotting scope is important enough to bring, even though it takes up some room.

Chad Schearer: It's not necessary to be too heavy on clothes. Many inexperienced elk hunters are accustomed to sitting in tree stands for long hours, but elk hunting is exercise and walking. I recommend that guys dress in layers, but leave the extra at home.

Van Hale: There's a lot of stuff out there that's made to sell and not to use. What ever happened to the days when we didn't even use a backpack? Now we've got so much gear we can't fit it all into a backpack. None of it comes to mind as being totally worthless, though I do think a lot of it is oversold.

Ross Johnson: Oh, there's a bunch of unnecessary, redundant stuff. Ninety percent of the hunters that come out have too much gear in their pack. Keep it simple. Hunters bring too many extra bullets, the heaviest rain gear they can find, and so on. I had a hunter from Alaska who was carrying a pack that weighed 80 pounds, and after the first day he told me, "I've got to get out of this Alaska syndrome. There's no place here I couldn't sleep out on the ground and survive with just one match."

Ron Dube: Well, there are all kinds of unnecessary gear that people bring to camp. If the client is not going to carry it himself, he's better off leaving it home. Most people bring too many clothes, too.

Rick Trusnovec: There's so much "supergear" out there nowadays, but none of it is absolutely worthless, I guess. I would say that the type of clothing some people wear is worthless for elk hunting. Fleece and wool is the way to go, and some of the high-tech stuff is just too darned noisy for hunting elk. Some of it may keep you a little drier, but it definitely is not as quiet as fleece and wool. I state in my mail-outs not to bring certain types of clothing. Inevitably, though, hunters bring it anyway.

Bob Fontana: There are lots of gadgets of questionable value out there these days. Where we hunt, even something like a rangefinder isn't very important. I've found that a lot of hunters who use rangefinders become too dependent on them. Even if they're shooting a flat-shooting centerfire rifle, they want to know the range all the time, whether it's 50 yards or 250 yards, and it makes absolutely no difference at those distances. If it's 400 or 500 yards, we almost never shoot at elk that far away anyway, because 300 yards is a long shot in our country. The high-tech, supposedly rainproof outerwear that some of the guys are bringing up is a real pain in the butt when you're elk hunting. You're going to get wet when you're elk hunting, either from rain or snow, or even frost or dew. I still find wool and polar fleece to be the best. So-called stealth cloth and Gore-Tex, especially in pants, are just too crinkly and noisy.

Brent Sinclair: There are a lot of worthless gadgets available. I've had guys come who, if they don't own it, it's only because

Cabela's doesn't sell it. Gadgets always seem to cost people opportunities. An example would be anything that makes noise or flashes, little compasses hanging here and there, or bells of some kind. I just tell the hunter, we won't need that, so just take it off. Gadgets to me include any item of equipment that isn't needed on an elk hunt.

Dave Fyfe: Part of the fun of hunting is all the stuff people buy, so I try not to take the fun out of it for them. But anything oversize to me is worthless. Guys come with oversize guns, oversize binoculars, oversize knives, oversize backpacks, stuff they can't handle. When I see a guy with a good, compact binocular, a gun he can handle, a sensible knife, I know I'm with a guy who has some experience. Oversize is so often overkill. Bigger is not always better in hunting.

Bill Perkins: A lot of people try to carry too much. A daypack with such necessities as a compass or GPS, a space blanket, fire starter materials, a map of the area, some energy food, and water are all that are absolutely necessary. This provides what you need to survive in the wilderness for a day or two if things should go wrong. Leave the pistols, the gadgets, and all the other gear behind; it just slows you down.

Chapter 6

HUNTING ON PRIVATE LAND FOR ELK

Featured Guides:
John Caid, White Mountain Apache Tribe, Arizona
Allen Morris, Three Forks Ranch, Colorado

Describe your home guiding area for elk.

John Caid: The White Mountain Apache Reservation is 1.7 million acres, and 1.2 million is our hunting area. The elevation ranges from almost 12,000 feet down to 5,000 feet, and even lower in places—from above timberline all the way down to the manzanita and piñon flats, where some of these bulls hang out. It's a pretty special and beautiful place.

Allen Morris: Three Forks Ranch is 200,000 total acres on the Colorado-Wyoming border, 40 miles north of Steamboat Springs, Colorado. We border the Routt National Forest on the south and the Medicine Bow National Forest on the north. We're surrounded on three sides by national forest, and we get elk coming in off there every day there's a hunting season. We've got more elk than Yellowstone National Park. On 15 October we'll have about 6,000 elk on the 70,000 acres in Colorado. It's easy to be good when you've got that many animals to choose from. We've got some of the finest elk hunting in the country. There were very few elk in this part of the country in 1980, but the elk population in Colorado has boomed. The grass up here is famous for nutrition, and yearling cattle will gain two to three pounds a day on it. The elk just do phenomenally well up here.

What are some distinctions that set it apart?

John Caid: Its size sets it apart, and the low number of hunters we have for an area this size. The age and composition

Is that an elk I see over there?

of the elk herd here is different than it is in most places. The average bull is 354 net and 365 gross. The average age of bulls taken is nine years, and we do take some up to thirteen years. It's a very old age class herd. The bull-to-cow ratio is very indicative of a trophy population, and we have one bull to every 2½ cows. That's a very high bull-to-cow ratio. The White Mountain Apache Tribe is on a draw system for tribal members for trophy bulls, and they hunt a 500,000-acre parcel that's reserved just for them. No nonmembers ever hunt there. They have to apply and be drawn in order to hunt, and their season is limited to two to three weeks.

Allen Morris: Ours is a unique hunting situation because we're hunting bulls that are 2½, 3½, and 4½ years old, but some of our cows are fourteen to fifteen years old. The cows are very mature, and they've played this game a lot. I manage the cows more than the bulls. Here the elk split, and some winter in

Colorado and some in Wyoming. The cows that winter in Wyoming eat grass that's a lot coarser, and they live only ten to twelve years before they wear their teeth out. Those that winter here in Colorado eat softer vegetation and some winter wheat, and they live up to fifteen years before they run out of teeth. For the last four to five years I've been calling more than ever because I've got to do more to fool those old cows into thinking there's another herd of elk over here, and it isn't a hunter.

So I take a different approach from most others. I know that if I can convince those cows that the grass is greener or they need to be where I'm at, the bulls will follow the cows. We're taught as kids to hunt all day and hunt hard, and you can do that with mule deer or antelope, and they'll just move around you. But if you don't let a cow elk lie down and chew her cud and nurse her calf, she'll change zip codes until she finds a place where she can. That's the big difference with elk—taking care of them and giving them their down time. If an elk has food and water, she'll stay put. The bulls think they run the show, but it's the lead cow that will take them out of the country if she's pushed too hard.

Why should a hunter hire a guide, as opposed to being self-guided?

John Caid: In a lot of cases hunters don't have time to get out and do the necessary scouting. The hunter hires the guide to get out and do the scouting for him. If a guy wants all the gratification he can get out of a hunt, and he has the time to take off three weeks to scout and talk to people in the area and gather information, great. But the guide has already spent that time out there and knows where to start in the morning, where they're going to be bugling, what routes they use to go up the ridges to bed down. Guides are a shortcut to gaining that knowledge.

Allen Morris: Some people will never hire a guide, just because they're hands-on, do-it-yourself guys. They're the kind of individuals who change their own oil and fix their own plumbing. There are other reasons people don't hire guides. I think a guy should hire a guide if he wants to learn. I'm not bragging, but we're the best at what we do, and for the last twenty years elk have consumed my whole life. I've learned a lot about calling them and being around them. I'll hunt every day from 1 September to 10 November, out in the field virtually every day. By doing that I get to watch the elk respond to my calling, react to my movements, and if a guy can hire me for five days he'll learn more about hunting elk than if he did it ten years by himself.

What is your success rate on trophy animals?

John Caid: We average just above 90 percent of our hunters taking animals. The ones who aren't successful have seen a lot of bulls, because you'll see twenty to twenty-five 6x6 bulls a day on the White Mountain Apache Reservation. A lot of our hunters have been hunting with us for twenty years, and if they don't see the right animal, they simply don't shoot.

Allen Morris: Last year we took sixty-five elk hunters, fifteen of whom were archery hunters. Fourteen of the archery hunters killed an elk, and the other one wounded an elk. All fifty of our rifle hunters killed an elk. Of those fifty elk, ten were over 300 inches. We were virtually 100 percent across the board. It's just because first, we have the animals, and second, we are the best at what we do.

Describe your usual hunting method and any common variations.

John Caid: Each guide on both the White Mountain and Havasupai Reservations has his own area. We divide the reservation up into three camps, which we operate simultaneously. They usually drive to the selected area, then get out and walk, following the bulls as they go from their morning feeding areas to their afternoon bedding areas. Generally, that's the pattern. Now, if they're moving a long ways, the guide may go back to the truck and take it around and get on top of where the bulls come up. We have some very distinctive areas that a guide who has been there for a while will recognize as a bedding area. They'll get in there, and the bulls will work their way to the top. That's where they pick them up again.

Allen Morris: I like to get up and eat a good breakfast, then access the ranch by truck, horse, four-wheeler, however. Right away we start working the animals. The difference that sets us apart is that we spend all our time actually hunting elk. A lot of elk hunters spend five to seven days just trying to find elk to hunt. We can spend less time looking for elk and more time hunting elk. And you have to know where those elk are living to do that. During September I'm trying to call those bulls.

We're in the Ranching for Wildlife program, so we get to start 1 September with any weapon—rifle, bow, crossbow, muzzleloader—any legal weapon. We can offer a rifle rut hunt in September, but it's almost criminal because that time of year it's easy to get within 100 yards of a bull elk if he's being very vocal. We work in on those elk, and I try to get my hunter as close as I can to the animal that he wants. Sometimes that means showing him several bulls before he finds the one he wants.

Archery hunters tend to be less picky about trophies, and we just try to call bulls in close all day every day until the thermals switch. Usually the elk are feeding in the meadows, working their way to bedding areas. Most always the feeding areas are below the bedding areas, so they're working their way into the quakies and out of the meadows toward the ridge where they'll lie down, chew their cud, and feed their babies. We get in behind them, and the wind is usually blowing downhill in the morning. Somewhere between 7:30 and 10:30 A.M. the valleys heat up and the wind will switch and start blowing back up. If that switch takes place and you're right in there, close to those elk, they're going to smell you. So we always get out before the thermal switches. They never even know you were there, and they'll stay in that general area. If you push it, and decide to call that bull in, knowing that any moment the thermal is going to switch, he will smell you. The cows will smell you, too, and I'm telling you, they can move out of that country simply because you stayed too long.

So I hunt primarily until I feel that thermal start to switch: I live by a puff bottle; when that wind isn't right, I'm out of there. I've been with hunters who have paid big bucks to hunt elk with me, and at 7:30 A.M. I'm walking back toward the vehicle. They're saying, "Wait a minute, I've only got five days to hunt and you're walking back to the truck at 7:30?" I've had people in total amazement. But I tell them, "Look, if you'll trust me on this, this afternoon at 3:00 we're going to sit right here and wait for those elk to come right down to us." Thirty minutes before dark the guy is standing over a six-point bull.

How do you hunt differently with a client/hunter, as opposed to when hunting alone (for yourself)?

John Caid: It depends on the physical characteristics of the hunter. If the hunter can't get around, we have to do it differently. If the hunter is in average shape, we do it a little differently. If a hunter can really move, then we go after it, and we go up and down and over, and we stay after them and pick up new bulls as we move. If it were just me, then I might be able to get around a little more. Our hunts are designed for the comfort and ability level of the hunter, so I probably wouldn't pack as much food and water if I were alone.

Allen Morris: I've started using a decoy over the past five years. I set one client thirty yards downwind, and I keep the other client within ten yards of me so I can communicate verbally with him. When I'm by myself I don't have that downwind leg, and I don't have two hunters to intercept bulls that come in at different angles. I still use the decoy, and I still do everything pretty much the same—except that I don't have the luxury of intercepting a bull that circles fifty yards away to get my wind. I don't have a client down there to zap him when he makes that corner. I don't call any differently, and I use the decoy about the same. Either way I'm trying to get that bull right in tight.

What time of season offers the best hunting in your area (and the highest possibility of success on trophy animals)?

John Caid: We start our hunts the second week of September, usually around the fifteenth. The very peak of the rut, when they're absolutely screaming and the bulls are totally insane, usually hits around 28 or maybe 29 September. Those are the times when you can walk into an area and they no longer even care if you're there. That's only happened four times in twenty-five years: when the bulls would come within ten feet of you. The cows are whining—they're downwind from you, they're upwind from you,

White Mountain Apache Reservation bull.

and you're right in the middle of them with no cover, but they don't care. They are rutting so hard and fighting so hard, it's the most awesome thing I've ever seen.

Allen Morris: If you're a rifle hunter, the best time is 15 September through 15 October. For archery hunting, I want to hunt the first ten days of September. I'll differ on this from most guys. I want to archery hunt those big bulls before they get in with the cows. I want to catch them while they're cruising and they've just rubbed off their velvet. After the bulls rub their velvet, they go through what's known as a sulky period of five to seven days, when they don't eat or sleep. When they rub their velvet they get a shot of testosterone that surges through their system, and it really shuts them down. Some bulls are affected for only a day or two, but I've seen some shut down for ten days.   When they come out of it, they're bulletproof and good looking. The only problem is there aren't any cows in estrus then—only 1 percent of the cows are in estrus by 30 August. So there aren't any cows to breed, their hormones are raging, and they start shredding trees.

I've killed sixteen elk with my bow, thirteen of them bulls, and I killed eight of those bulls on 8 September. Give me the first ten days of September, and I'll kill more and bigger bulls than the other twenty days of September. The reason I think I'm more successful then is that they're not in with the cows. They don't call as much because they're not very vocal—they won't even let you know they're coming. They will come to a call and investigate to see if this cow is in estrus, because she sounds like she is, and what's this small bull doing already trying to breed her? They have a pecking order, and they do not want smaller bulls breeding the cows. Those big bulls are really active, cruising to see which herd of cows they want to set in with. They're at their most vulnerable point; in fact, all bulls are vulnerable during the first ten days of September. Some people skip those ten days because they want to hear the bugling and carrying on that takes place from the fifteenth to the twenty-fifth, but I think they're missing the boat. The best time to kill a big bull elk is the first ten days of September.

Allen Morris and client with a great Colorado bull.

How much does weather influence the hunting success in your area?

John Caid: If it's hot and dry the way it often is in Arizona, the bugling will shut down a little earlier. Activity may just be really early in the morning, maybe even before sunup, and they don't start back up until late, sometimes after dark. Cold, wet weather—and though most people don't know it, Arizona has some of that—certainly peaks the rut. You can see the rut picking up. I love rainfall while we're hunting, because it knocks down the scent, makes it quieter to get around, and elk don't seem to hear as well. The moon phase is important, too—when there's a full moon, those bulls are active all night long, and they shut down during the day.

Allen Morris: I've been in 90-degree heat the first ten days of September, and in twelve inches of snow. Those elk are going to do what they're going to do, and the rut is going to dictate how they react. Of course, if it's really bad weather, and it's just pouring rain or snowing, it's miserable on the hunters. But the elk are still out there doing their thing. They won't come roaring in to a call as easily, and the percentages are going to go down. But the elk still have to live, they've still got to eat, they've still got to sleep, and the rut still interests them. Inclement weather affects hunters more than it does elk.

How much does weather and time of season influence where and how you hunt in your area?

John Caid: When it's hot and dry, we try to get out even earlier and find out where the bulls are. They may be on their way up the mountain already by daylight, especially if it's hot and dry and there's a full moon. At such times they may not be active at all during the day, so we'll change our hunt pattern a little and try to catch them in their beds. We have to spend more time just trying to locate them. During times like those we generally stay out in our spike camp, which is right in the middle of our hunting area, an hour and a half from the main camp. During a poor weather year, that is important in case the elk do pick up in the middle of the day—which they might. Sometimes we just stay out there all day long instead of coming in after the morning hunt.

Allen Morris: The first ten days of September I'll do a lot of rattling, soft calling, and so forth, and I'll stay on stand forty-five minutes, waiting for those bulls to come in silently. As soon as the bulls set in with the cows, I completely change tactics. I go to managing the cows and hunting the herds. It becomes a total challenge to get in close, because instead of one or two sets of eyes, you've got fifty or sixty or more. So you've got to change your tactics. You've got to be stealthier, and you've got to be a little slicker in how you move around. When you get in close you've got all those noses, so you've got to really pay attention to the wind. Once 15 October comes around, the bulls are pulling away from the cows, and I think a post-rut bull elk has to be one of the toughest animals to hunt. He doesn't call, and you almost have to hunt him like you do big mule deer: strictly spot-and-stalk. So time of season completely influences how I hunt.

Chapter 7

PUBLIC LAND GUIDES, NORTHERN ROCKIES

Featured Guides:
Jack Atcheson Jr., Jack Atcheson & Sons, Montana
Chad Schearer, Central Montana Outfitters, Montana

Describe your home guiding area for elk.

Jack Atcheson Jr.: I've guided all of the Missouri and Powder River breaks, as well as the wilderness areas north of Yellowstone. I've guided most of southwest Montana, in fact.

Chad Schearer: I hunt central Montana, a place that isn't high elevation, but it's steep country. It's a really good area with a lot of water.

What are some distinctions that set it apart?

Jack Atcheson Jr.: It's distinctive because of sheer elk numbers, but also because the elk around Yellowstone were never wiped out and they're very much indigenous. There's a very liberal season that starts on 1 September, and in some areas you can hunt all the way into early March. You can hunt elk in high alpine areas early, and then hunt them on snowshoes during the late seasons. There haven't been a lot of those kinds of hunts around in the past.

Chad Schearer: There are no cattle on the land, so the livestock factor is removed. I think that's an important distinction.

Why should a hunter hire a guide, as opposed to being self-guided?

Jack Atcheson Jr.: The hunter gets a lot more out of the trip when he's guided. Odds of success may double or triple. For an unguided hunter, resident and nonresident, the success rate overall is about 15 percent. A good outfitter can have your odds up around 50 percent on most public land hunts. It's like paying for your own education. You go with an outfitter for one or two trips, and you can get qualified to do it on your own if you choose. But most hunters who go with an outfitter come to realize that this guy's up at 3:00 A.M. taking care of the horses and so on. When we come home at night, the hunter is free to go directly into the tent to swap stories, but the outfitter still has to unsaddle horses, hang meat, or cook dinner. An outfitter removes a lot of hurdles that could wear a guy down; he lets a hunter enjoy the finer aspects of going on a hunting trip.

Jack Atcheson Jr. with a very nice Montana bull.

Elk country.

Chad Schearer: When you go with an outfitter, he's going to have the equipment in place, and he should have a pretty good idea of where the elk are and what they're doing. If you're going self-guided, you're going to need a lot more time because you may spend the first week just trying to locate the elk. If you're on a guided hunt, you're pretty much going to spend all your time hunting—at least that's what you should be doing. If a guy has a month off, he can get by self-guided, but I'd recommend he go up in the summertime before the season and spend some time learning the area.

What is your success rate on trophy animals?

Jack Atcheson Jr.: On my backpack hunts I had 100 percent success on six-point bulls. We took it to them and hunted hard.

If we went horseback, it was probably 50 to 60 percent being five- and six-point bulls. On the snowshoe hunts in December, the weather made a big difference. Sometimes I could show a guy fifty to sixty bulls in one herd, but then the next hunt it would get mild and the elk would go away up high: The good days were very good, and the bad days—well, we won't talk about them.

Chad Schearer: Success rate really depends on the year and the weather and the season. The bulls we typically take are good-quality five- and six-pointers in the 300-point range. Guys in good shape who can shoot straight have a higher success rate, naturally, but you don't always get the ideal hunter.

Describe your usual hunting method and any common variations.

Jack Atcheson Jr.: You have to remember that an elk may range three or four miles between where he feeds and where he

A snowy wilderness camp scene.

Chad Schearer with a beautiful bull taken among Rocky Mountain quakies.

beds. It's nothing for an elk to stand up in his bed at 10,000 feet, and in an hour he's three or four miles away down in some meadow or hay bottom. I like to get at a real good vantage point, particularly in the evening, and study areas with a spotting scope at great distances where old bulls might come out of the timber to feed. You have to use a binocular and a spotting scope a lot. When elk are active and there's snow on the ground, you can see tracks and sign and where elk have dug with their front feet to make feeding craters. A lot of times they'll go back to those same spots to feed. That's a good way to find the big bulls. In the big herds you don't normally find big bulls, but mostly raghorns and cows. I like to let my eyes do the walking, because I know my legs aren't going to be able to do as much as my eyes.

Chad Schearer: One thing I've been doing a lot lately is educating archers about the kinds of bulls we're hunting today. In fact, some of the seminars I've been doing lately have been entitled "Call Less for More Bulls." We've got a lot of educated bulls that are harder to call in and are a lot more wary. I listen a

111

lot more than I used to, instead of doing locater calls. Sometimes I get out there at 2:00 or 3:00 A.M., if I've got a full moon, and I listen, just trying to locate the elk. When it gets legal shooting time we try to call them in. I've had situations in which I've cow-called only three times over a period of an hour, and we harvested the bull. Before, the method was to call them aggressively, so as to get them fired up and screaming. Today I call less and try to blow the right call at the right time. When I'm rifle hunting, I like to get up real high and real early and find them going from their feeding grounds into their bedding area. I like to watch them move, and once they bed down I try to move in on them and get in as close as I can. During rifle season I like to do a lot of glassing.

How do you hunt differently with a client/hunter, as opposed to when hunting alone (for yourself)?

Jack Atcheson Jr.: I'd say that the main difference is assessing what my hunter can do, because what the hunter can do is what you can do when you're guiding. You sometimes have to take the easy routes and minimize the physical activity because of your hunter. That's not a problem hunting alone.

Chad Schearer: With a client hunter you have more noise going through the woods. One of my guides, Ricky Hooters, came up with a saying: "The client is the weapon." Basically, when you're hunting with that client, he's your gun, he's your bow, or whatever. If that weapon is not with you, you're not going to be able to get your animal. So when I'm out hunting with a client, it doesn't matter if I can get up to where the elk are. If my client can't get there to finish the job, there's no way to make it happen. When I'm with a client I have to go at his speed and watch his physical capabilities. That's not a problem when I'm alone.

What time of season offers the best hunting in your area (and the highest possibility of success on trophy animals)?

Jack Atcheson Jr.: Right now in Montana archers have the best opportunity of all. Hunting late September or early October with a bow is absolutely the most opportune time to take a mature bull elk. The opening week of big game season at the end of October can be quite good for big bulls, too. Migratory options really don't happen until about the end of November, if it even happens at all.

Chad Schearer: We're in an area that has resident animals. I personally feel that bowhunting gives us the best possibility for the largest animals, because it's during the rut.

How much does weather influence the hunting success in your area?

Jack Atcheson Jr.: We don't have the weather we used to have, and it's changed hunting in Montana. We still have a lot of bull hunters hunting the late season, but we just don't have much winter weather in November. It takes 18 inches of snow to move an elk, and then he drops down to where it's 17 inches deep. You need days of subzero cold, 20 to 30 below zero, winds, and many feet of snow, and then it really catches an elk's attention. If you don't have that, or if you're gambling on that and you don't get it, you're not going to see any migration at all.

Chad Schearer: Weather affects elk hunting no matter where you're hunting. In hot weather they will act differently, as they will with wind, snow, or whatever. The biggest thing I've found is that you change your tactics. Out of thirty days of elk hunting, no matter where I hunt, I figure there are going to be about four or five days that are just ideal for hunting elk. There will probably be about ten days that are good but not ideal. There are going to be about ten days that are not that great. And there are going to be about five days that are just plain poor. When you're guiding and hunting every day, you've got to get out there and make things happen regardless. For example, on really windy days elk are going to be a lot spookier, and they're going to be hanging out in heavy timber. In hot, dry weather I'm going to be looking for the water holes. If I find a water hole, I'll even take a rake into an area and rake the ground down so I know that these elk are coming in late or early or whatever, and I can see how

Author approaches a fallen elk.

much fresh activity there's been. Basically, I try to be a rubber band and stretch into the different hunting techniques that I need to use in order to be successful.

How much does weather and time of season influence where and how you hunt in your area?

Jack Atcheson Jr.: If it's a warm, dry season, then you've got to take it to the elk in higher country. Higher country in a lot of southwest Montana is reached by going only three or four miles; it's not like taking a twenty-mile horseback ride. You get into these dark, deep basins, these black holes as we call them, where it's super heavy timber, the kind elk need for security and cover. Expect the animals at that altitude not to be feeding much in the daylight, just a little early in the morning and in the evening. They remain bedded in those black timber holes until cooler weather, because they're wearing a pretty heavy coat.

Chad Schearer: Weather does affect how I hunt. If it's dry and crunchy, you have to be careful where you walk. If it's snowing, that's another thing that changes our tactics. If it gets below zero, the elk are going to be hanging around in conifer patches where there's thick timber for insulation, and where it's a little warmer. They even go from grazing to browsing. If it's a full moon, they often bed an hour or two before sunrise, but then they'll be moving an hour or two earlier in the afternoon.

Chapter 8

PUBLIC LAND GUIDES, DESERT SOUTHWEST

Featured Guides:
Van Hale, Trophy Outfitters, Arizona
Ross Johnson, Ross Johnson Outfitters, New Mexico

Describe your home guiding area for elk.

Van Hale: Our elevation is from 6,500 to 9,000 feet. Our guiding area is in the White Mountains of Arizona and the Gila Mountains of New Mexico. We have a huge variety of country here, everything from rolling sagebrush plains to piñon-juniper forest to aspen high country. I've been all over, and this area has some of the greatest variety of terrain I've ever seen. Some of the areas in which we hunt these bulls are almost treeless, and we've even got some huge open spaces where some of the big bulls live. There are a lot of draws that go clear up to 9,000 feet into the dark aspens, and sometimes the animals are holed up there.

Ross Johnson: We're in the desert Southwest, basically piñon/juniper with scattered ponderosa pine. The elevation is 6,000 to 8,000 feet in high plains country. We hunt the edge more than anything.

What are some distinctions that set it apart?

Van Hale: The distinction here would have to be the quality of elk, because we've got some of the biggest elk in the country.

Ross Johnson: It's a reverse situation from most elk country, as far as where the elk are at different times. One big mistake that hunters make here in the Southwest, maybe from reading magazines, is that you've got to be up in the quaking aspen trees to bugle in an elk. That's because magazine articles tend to tell you to go high to hunt the rut, but what they're describing is the Wyoming-Montana country. In the Southwest the elk do go high in winter, but you're hunting in September and October, and at that time all the elk are down low. They're in the edge of the plains, in the piñon/juniper; they're in the flat country. Some of these elk never do come into the trees. A lot of them go out onto the prairies at night and then go in to within a mile or so of the edge of the timber and bed down. In most of this country it's that way—kind of backwards from other places. The only time we see elk up high is during winter.

Why should a hunter hire a guide, as opposed to being self-guided?

Van Hale: If you're coming all the way to Arizona or New Mexico to hunt elk, you need to hire a guide to get the most

Ross Johnson with a happy hunter.

Van Hale and a magnificent high-desert bull.

out of it. The travel and other expenses will amount to quite a bit of money, and chances of success are at least doubled by hiring a guide. There are a lot of do-it-yourselfers out there who don't want to hire a guide, and that's great, but realistically most guys can't come a week or ten days before their hunt to scout and find the elk. A lot of guys come out and hunt without a guide, and by the time they figure out where the elk are, it's time to head home.

Ross Johnson: There's a kind of hunter who is really good at it, and who has the time and experience, and who can go out and kill an elk on his own. He doesn't need me. But there are business people for whom time is money, and they don't want to have to put up with cooking for themselves, skinning the animal, getting it to the taxidermist or meat processor, or whatever. They also don't have time to come out and scout two weeks ahead of time. That's where I come in.

What is your success rate on trophy animals?

Van Hale: Our success rate is really good. On the rifle hunts for the past several years our kill rate has been about 80 percent, about 70 percent on muzzleloader hunts, and about 50 percent on archery. Some of those bulls are huge, too, including a 417 B&C bull last year, and a 379 this year.

Ross Johnson: That depends on what people call a trophy. We pass up far more elk than we kill. We've gotten into the market of 350–400 class bulls, so there are a lot of outfitters who are shooting elk that we don't shoot at all. In our world, as far as a trophy is concerned, it's got to be a B&C elk. I've particularly gotten in on the hunt for the Arizona and New Mexico governors' permits for elk the last four or five years, and in those cases it's got to score 400+ or it's not a trophy. But really, I think "trophy" depends on the hunter. I think some of the most excited hunters I've ever seen in my life are the first-timers who have saved for a long time to do a hunt, and they come out and shoot an elk. It might be just a 280 bull and maybe they shot it with a bow. They don't care what it measures—they're the most excited people you'll ever see. On the other hand, I've seen people shoot 400-class bulls and tip the guide $1,000, but they're not even excited. Instead, they're standing around waiting on the tape measure to see if it really makes the 400 mark. Whether it's a trophy or not is all tied up with the hunter's expectations.

Describe your usual hunting method and any common variations.

Van Hale: That depends. During archery season we're calling during the rut, or sitting on a tree stand in the evenings. Once we get into the muzzleloader and rifle hunts in October, we still do some calling, but we tend toward a lot more glassing. As it gets into November and December, it becomes all glassing. We spend a lot of time looking up into big canyons where we can glass bulls on the southern slopes of their winter range. That time of year we often have to shoot across the canyon from one side to the other.

Ross Johnson: We normally use spot-and-stalk, and we also have some tree stands and some water hole stands. We use a little calling, but it's very dependent on the situation. Here in this part of the world there are big bulls, and the ones that have the most cows are mostly in the 375 to 380 B&C class. Your 400-class bulls usually grab four or five cows and leave. If we're hunting a bull like that, we normally use no calling at all. Basically, we use no calling for the biggest bulls, even those in the 375 class. The smaller bulls, 350 and less—you can call them and fool with them all day. If you're going to call in one of these big bulls, in the 390 to 400 class, you pretty well have to get into his world and understand his day-to-day life before you have any chance using a call.

How do you hunt differently with a client/hunter, as opposed to when hunting alone (for yourself)?

Van Hale: The only thing I do differently with a client is that I don't cover as much ground. Generally I don't do very much differently. How you hunt with a particular client depends on his capabilities. If the guy is really noisy or physically unfit, and you just can't get him through the woods, then you're going to have to change your tactics to sitting in meadows and trying to let the elk come to you instead of going to them. You have to customize the hunt to the client.

Ross Johnson: I don't do any hunting on my own. If I did, the difference would be the ability to go and not be physically handicapped by having someone else along. I'd be able to cover the country better and have the patience to wait out whatever situation came up.

What time of season offers the best hunting in your area (and the highest possibility of success on trophy animals)?

Van Hale: Our October hunts are our most successful ones, coming right at the tail end of the rut but in rifle or muzzleloader season. Archery season is during the rut, and while our success rate is only 50 percent, about 90 percent get a shot.

Ross Johnson: Best hunting is during the rut in September, and then very late, in December. Those are my favorite times. I can't say for sure which is better, but I prefer the late hunt. In December the bulls around here go high and hang out in little bachelor groups. Two of our governor's permit hunters have killed 400+ bulls in December. The animals are more vulnerable then than at any other time, because they hang out together and they're not keyed up by the rut. The rut really energizes these elk. It's not so much the bulls but all those cows, with so many pairs of eyes, that make the rut a challenge. There's no question you see more 400-class elk during the rut, but taking them is another matter. And while I prefer the late hunt for actually killing a big bull, I believe the rut is the most fun time to hunt.

How much does weather influence the hunting success in your area?

Van Hale: Greatly. That's the outfitter's greatest crutch, because we can always say it's too hot or too dry or it rained all week, or whatever. Realistically, weather's one thing that's out of our control, but it can definitely make or break a hunt—absolutely.

Ross Johnson: Medium. Elk are generally fair-weather animals. They don't like a lot of wind and bad weather, unlike mule deer, where the worse it gets the better the hunting. It does affect elk, but we never have that much bad weather in this area, anyway. Most of the time it's 70 to 80 degrees while you're hunting.

How much does weather and time of season influence where and how you hunt in your area?

Van Hale: You definitely hunt differently in different conditions. For example, take our November rifle hunt in Arizona. If we have a lot of snow up top, those bulls all migrate down to lower country, so that's where you're going to be hunting. If it doesn't snow, then you're going to be way up top. The weather will dictate to a tremendous degree how you're going to hunt and where you're going to hunt.

Ross Johnson: Weather and season don't influence us much. Here there's no migration, because these are resident elk. Since they don't move around much, it's not much of a factor.

Chapter 9

WILDERNESS GUIDES, U.S.A.

Featured Guides:
Ron Dube, Ron Dube's Wilderness Adventures, Wyoming
Rick Trusnovec, Horse Creek Outfitters, Idaho

Describe your home guiding area for elk.

Ron Dube: My camp is twenty-four miles by horseback from the end of the road. You have to go through five miles of Yellowstone National Park to access my camp. I'm the only outfitter in the world that I know of who has a permit to transport firearms through a national park to get to a hunting area outside the park. The camp is a mile and a half from the east boundary of Yellowstone. There are 30,000 elk that summer in Yellowstone. Not all of those elk are available to us, of course, but there are a significant number of animals there that live close to the boundary and are part of our local elk herd. We have a regular weekly or daily recruitment of fresh elk that haven't been chased before, nor have they smelled or heard people. They are quite wild but not as sophisticated as elk that have no way to escape from hunting pressure. Plus, I have a long hunting season and minimal hunting pressure from people outside our camp.

Rick Trusnovec: We're in the Frank Church "River of No Return" Wilderness Area, which is the biggest wilderness in the Lower Forty-eight, almost 2.4 million acres. We operate totally in the Frank Church Area. We take in the first twelve to fourteen miles of the Selway, and we come close to the Selway-Bitterroot Wilderness boundary, but that's outside our area. We operate in two units, and on the other side we go down to the Salmon River. Our area is basically twenty by twenty-five miles. There's still country that we haven't penetrated in the eleven years of our operation here. It's virgin wilderness with no roads and nothing motorized, period. The only access is by horseback or walking.

What are some distinctions that set it apart?

Ron Dube: This hunting area goes back to the early 1900s. It's been an outfitter camp for a long, long time. At one time the National Park Service and Wyoming Game and Fish were transporting grizzly bears into our area because it's so remote and it's a dynamite habitat. It is high, with an elevation of 8,600 feet. Even in drought conditions the grass is green up here until hard frost because of all the springs and lots of high, above-timber snowbanks. These are a kind of reservoir. They don't melt in a year's time but just get added onto when we get more winter snowfall. That keeps the springs alive and keeps the vegetation green, so it's a real magnet for wildlife.

Rick Trusnovec: The sheer size of the wilderness area, which means lack of people, is what sets it apart. There are not many areas like it left in the Lower Forty-eight. I spend three and a half to four months out there, and all this fall I didn't see a single person who wasn't part of our camp.

Why should a hunter hire a guide, as opposed to being self-guided?

Ron Dube: Guides are required in Wyoming for wilderness hunts, except for Wyoming residents. We get a significant number of Wyoming residents hunting in our area as clients, because we supply the horses and the knowledge of the area. As anyone who regularly hunts these animals must realize, elk live in little pieces of microhabitat. They don't inhabit the whole range at any one time. If you can pick out the hotspots where the elk are apt to be, it minimizes the amount of time it takes to find them. Since we've been guiding here for sixteen years, and have thirty years of elk hunting experience, we can help people be more successful in killing larger elk in a shorter time. Many people, residents or not, don't have the horses and equipment, nor the knowledge of the country and habits of its

One never tires of looking at remote wilderness scenery, which is pleasing to the eyes.

game, to be successful as quickly as they can be if they hire somebody like us.

Rick Trusnovec: You've got to travel if you're going to get way back away from roads. Where we operate we travel some five hours by horseback. The private individual, to get way back in there, is going to take away from his own hunting time. He's got to take enough stock with him, and in addition do all the chores. What the hunter is really there for is to hunt and try to harvest a bull, not take care of horses and do camp work. Some people just love to be there and do all that, I guess. But most people don't have all that time to lose pulling trucks with trailers and doing the other work. If a guy has done that before and tries it with us one time, he'll never go back to doing it for himself.

What is your success rate on trophy animals?

Ron Dube: The average elk that my clients kill is 5½ points, that meaning it's a 5x6. More than 50 percent of the elk we kill are 6x6. I would say the average size of the elk we kill is 280 or 290 Boone and Crockett points. We kill elk that score better than 340 every fall. We kill elk occasionally that break 370, including one three years ago that scored 374. We kill very few raghorns, only one or two a year. Our kill percentage is somewhere between 70 and 75 percent in an average year. Opportunity for our hunters to kill branch-antlered bulls is 90 to 95 percent. Some years 100 percent of our forty clients have an opportunity to kill a five- or six-point bull in the course of our eight-day hunt (six days of hunting, and a day in and a day out).

Rick Trusnovec: That gets down to what you mean by "trophy animal." We usually take elk for 40 to 50 percent of our hunters. As far as legitimate opportunity, we run 65 to 70 percent, and unfortunately sometimes the hunter either can't hit the animal, or he's a trophy hunter and turns down the bull because it isn't big enough.

Describe your usual hunting method and any common variations.

Ron Dube: We generally get up a couple of hours before daylight, have breakfast, and the guides saddle the horses. Quite often we leave camp an hour or so before daylight to get to a spot where we think we might find elk at dawn. Most of the time we stay out all day and hunt hard. The elk are there twenty-four hours a day, and we tell people that. We hunt until it's too dark to shoot, and then we come back to camp. We keep doing that until the hunt's over or we're successful. We sometimes return to camp in the early part of the day if we feel the area we're hunting is not the best one at that particular time. If that happens we reevaluate and make another evening hunt. Quite often elk are active during the daytime, depending on weather and other conditions. We're subject to some migration later in the season, so if we get cold weather and snow we have fresh elk that are moving in the middle of the day all day long. We sometimes use tracking methods. I found that big bull I talked about earlier at 8:30 A.M. We followed him all day and killed him at 4:30 P.M. We also do a lot of bugling throughout the whole season, which is 1 September through 21 October. I have called in five- and six-point bulls the last two days of the season. I believe that's because cows that got missed in September come back into estrus twenty-six days later. When bulls think that there's a cow available, they bugle more. A lot of these elk were probably inside the park earlier in the season, and they're more susceptible to calling than elk that have been hunted all fall.

Rick Trusnovec: Hunting method varies throughout the year. In September on our rifle bugle hunts, which we still have in Idaho, you're out trying to locate bugling bulls or cows talking. It's such a game, learning about the species you're

Elk country.

hunting. Not every bull you locate is going to just fog over and charge right in, saying, "Here I am, take me!" A lot depends on what you do after you've located the animal. There are times when you sit and wait and keep bugling, and there are times when you take off after a bull because he's grabbing his cows and taking off. There are other times you just shut up and wait. There are a million different situations, and it takes experience to know what to do. There are times when you're tempted to go after a bull when the wind's not right, maybe because of pressure from the client. You will never kill a bull if the wind's not right—period. Too many guides, inexperienced or what have you, will let their hunter push them to go after that bull when the wind is wrong, or maybe the bull just isn't ready. When we leave camp in the morning darkness in September and early October, we may need to ride for an hour or two to get to the place we want to hunt that day. We bugle off vantage points looking to get a response. You also look for sign, tracks, and so on, working ridgetops as you try to locate elk. As it gets to mid-October and later, we change to a lot of glassing, because the weather is cooler and there may be some snow on the ground, and the elk are moving more. You get on a vantage point and do a lot of glassing, locate a bull your client is willing to go after, and then you figure out your sneak from there.

How do you hunt differently with a client/hunter, as opposed to when hunting alone (for yourself)?

Ron Dube: I hunt the late November season, after all my clients have gone home. Most of the time I shoot cows as long as I have a tag for "any elk," because at this time in my life I prefer not to shoot 300- to 325-point bulls. The only bull I'd be interested in would score 340 or better. Sometimes I get a second cow permit here in Wyoming, so I shoot two cows. If I had my druthers and weren't outfitting, I'd go into the high country in September, and I'd just keep looking for that big bull using bugling techniques. Many times you can stalk and shoot elk even if they won't come to you.

Rick Trusnovec: I don't get a chance to hunt for myself! In the last eleven years, since we've been outfitting, I've harvested one little spike bull. That's about all I've even picked up a gun to hunt. I just don't have the time. If I did have the time, on my own, I'd do a good part of it the same way I do it with clients. By myself, I could probably get a lot closer than I can with a client, because of the noise. With a client you often stop short and try to get a little bit longer shot, because unfortunately some clients can be noisy. I'd go anywhere with certain clients. There are others where it just would never happen.

What time of season offers the best hunting in your area (and the highest possibility of success on trophy animals)?

Ron Dube: It's very difficult to give you a definitive answer to that. Fifteen years ago the bulls bugled more aggressively

Rick Trusnovec with a good elk.

Ron Dube with a Wyoming wilderness bull.

when the rifle season opened on 10 September, so we killed some big bulls then. We also got good bulls at the end of the season, when we'd get the right weather and they'd drift out of the park to go to winter range. But if it's really windy, the wind is squirrely, or the snow gets crunchy, the elk would smell or hear you a long way off. That makes it difficult. For whatever reason, in the last few years our early-season hunting has been tougher—that is, we've had fewer opportunities, but we've been having more opportunities on bigger bulls the last couple of weeks of the season. I think if we analyzed data over a hundred-year period we'd probably come to the conclusion that every year is a little bit different.

Rick Trusnovec: Our September rifle opener during the rut is probably one of the best times to hunt. We also have a mid-October rifle opener in our other unit, and that's often the best hunt of the season for trophy game. We've taken a number of 340-class bulls on that hunt. We actually have three season openers. We bow hunt the whole month of September on the Salmon River side of our area, and then that unit shuts down for a while. Mid-September, we have our rifle opener during the rut on the Selway side, so we do three hunts out of that side until October 9. Then we go back over to the Salmon River side, where we have another opener for rifle season on October 15; that's the one that's often so darned good.

How much does weather influence the hunting success in your area?

Ron Dube: Weather is not as big a factor as most people would expect. We've had good luck on the later hunts in October, whether it was cold and snowy or not. Hunting conditions, I think, are more important than actual weather. If you have a lot of snow and it melts in the daytime, freezes at night, and stays crunchy all day long, it's very difficult to slip up on an elk. If the wind is blowing constantly, as it did in 1991, conditions can be so bad that it's very difficult to hunt. It's pretty tough to hunt in a blizzard. However, I don't subscribe to the notion that the weather is as important a factor as some people believe. Now, yes, when it's hot and dry, the elk aren't as active, and success is going to be down. Everybody will tell you that with early snow that's not crunchy, and lots of it, success is going to be high because tracking is so good. I would not cancel my hunt because I thought it was too warm or too cold, though. I think the main reason that people are unsuccessful is that they hunt in the wrong place. Hunter success on elk is more dependent on which state you're hunting and what time of year it is: Success is in the low 20s in some places, but between 80 and 90 percent on guided wilderness hunts in Wyoming. That's because there are lots of elk here, and also because of the perseverance of the guide and the client.

Rick Trusnovec: Early in the season the weather has a huge influence on success. No matter how good we think we are at what we do or how much experience we have, sometimes we get humbled, no matter how hard we hunt, no matter how far we ride. Usually it's because it's miserably hot. On our Selway side we had some huge fires a couple of years ago, and some people think that should make the hunting better. But when it's hot, the elk will be down in those deepest, darkest holes, and most of the time they just won't talk. If you go bailing off into one of those holes, all you're going to hear is crashing timber as the elk vacate. So hot weather is a killer. Late in the season, with cold weather and snow on the ground, game's all over the place and moving. If it's 70 degrees in November, then game isn't moving, and again that's tough. There's no question that in the wilderness, weather is the biggest factor in hunter success.

How much does weather and time of season influence where and how you hunt in your area?

Ron Dube: Now, that's a big factor. In October, when we usually start getting some significant amounts of snow, the elk are thinking about migrating to winter range anyway. In our particular case, when we get early snow it makes hunting conditions a lot easier because there are more elk available. Location has the same importance in a hunting camp as it does in commercial real estate: Location is crucial. Biologists will tell you that the most important factor in quality game areas is habitat. If you have quality habitat, you have large populations of game animals. Another big factor is minimal hunting pressure. Elk must feel safe to move freely.

Rick Trusnovec: Weather influences hunting an awful lot. We've had a lot of fires in our area over the years, and that's good for elk. When it's hot and dry, though, those elk aren't going to be in the middle of those burns on south-facing slopes the way they will when it's cool, so don't even waste your time going there. They're going to be somewhere else. The weather makes all the difference in the world as to where I'm going to be hunting that week.

Chapter 10

CANADIAN ROCKIES GUIDES

Featured Guides:
Bob Fontana, Elk Valley Bighorn Outfitters, British Columbia
Brent Sinclair, Porcupine Creek Outfitters, Alberta

Describe your home guiding area for elk.

Bob Fontana: Southeastern British Columbia is tremendously scenic. We're right in the heart of the Canadian Rockies. My guiding area is about sixteen miles due south and west of Banff National Park, so it's some of the most dramatically scenic country in the world. We hunt pretty big country, with some of the side drainages being anywhere from five to twenty-five miles long. We hunt them everywhere in that terrain, from the river bottoms and bench country up into the avalanche chutes and park-type areas that are common there. It's true elk country, where people like Teddy Roosevelt hunted in the past.

Brent Sinclair: I'm in the foothills, right at the base of the Rockies in Alberta. A lot of this country is ranchland with grain and hay parcels adjacent to foothills, where there is green timber. It's a boreal-type forest with lots of aspen and evergreens. Other parts of it go up into high alpine basins. There is really quite a diversity of terrains within a fifteen- to twenty-mile radius of where I am right now. Some of it is grassland, where the elk at times mix with cattle.

What are some distinctions that set it apart?

Bob Fontana: A major distinction is found in some of our management regimens, which are unique. We have a six-point-only rule in place throughout. The early rifle season starts on 10 September, and it's not very long, ending on 20 October. We get to chase the elk only during the rut and a little bit thereafter. We don't hammer them during the migration, which is a good thing in my mind. If you hunt them during the rut, then you should give them a rest afterward. With the present management regime, there's a real elk explosion going on here right now, with about thirty-five to forty bulls per hundred cows after the season. You usually don't see big herds in our area. If you see five or six elk together, there's probably a mature six-point bull in there with

Brent Sinclair with a trophy Alberta bull.

them, because the bull-to-cow ratio is so good. The other distinction is that we can hunt with rifles during the rut.

Brent Sinclair: As far as distinctions go, people mention most often that you've got antelope country, elk country, and bighorn sheep country within a twenty-mile drive of each other. You come off the shortgrass plains of southern Alberta and you hit the high Rockies abruptly, with a really narrow band of foothills.

Why should a hunter hire a guide, as opposed to being self-guided?

Bob Fontana: Knowing the area and hunting techniques is the reason. There are lots of elk hunters, but there aren't very many good ones, especially during the rut. It takes time and experience and a thorough knowledge of the area to figure out how to harvest those big bulls.

Brent Sinclair: The answer to that question has a lot to do with knowing the terrain and being able to maximize the time spent actually hunting. Elk in this part of the country are habituated to certain parcels of terrain, and some of it looks like elk country and some of it doesn't. The guide does all the footwork and has all the pieces in place before you arrive, so you don't have to spend much time trying to locate the elk.

What is your success rate on trophy animals?

Bob Fontana: Seventy-five percent. All of them would be six-point bulls or better.

Brent Sinclair: I guess I'd like to define what I feel a trophy elk is. I've had clients on their first elk hunt, and some of those people are archery hunters. Any legal bull called into bow range and harvested by a quick and humane kill is a trophy in my view. I have had clients take big 6x6 bulls at 200+ yards with a well-placed bullet from a scoped rifle when the bull never knew what happened, and those are also trophy elk. To me the meaning of the word "trophy" is what it means to the person who harvests the animal, as well as signifying what went into getting the animal. On archery, we have 100 percent shooting opportunity on 4x4, 5x5, and 6x6 bulls. I have four archery tags. With rifle hunting it's also 100 percent opportunity most of the time, though that depends on the size the client is willing to harvest. We don't advertise 350-class bulls for every hunter; we just advertise good, quality hunts with a high success rate in a good camp amid spectacular scenery.

Describe your usual hunting method and any common variations.

Bob Fontana: We hunt spot-and-stalk, using calls regularly to locate elk when we can't see them. We then get in and get dirty with them when we do find them.

Brent Sinclair: We like to get in where the elk are, where we know they are, and we move in slowly and set up and do a little cow calling. We may bugle a little. Once you've located elk

Bob Fontana and Curt Blankeny with a great British Columbia bull.

either vocally or visually, you get into that area as close as you can and use a cow call to try to get the bulls to come to you. We hit a lot of ridges, walk a lot of ridges, and glass so that we can locate the elk. In late winter we've got a few places where we can locate elk by glassing, and there we go in without any calling after we've spotted elk. So it's spot, stalk, call, or a combination.

How do you hunt differently with a client/hunter, as opposed to when hunting alone (for yourself)?

Bob Fontana: I wish I had a chance to hunt elk for myself these days. The advantage with a client is that you have someone getting ready to shoot while you're calling or looking or whatever. If you're hunting alone, you've got a diaphragm in your mouth and a binocular around your neck and you're trying to get your gun up to shoot this big bull: It becomes a bit problematic.

Brent Sinclair: I really don't do anything differently, except that with a client I'm going to gear my level of exertion to the client's abilities. If I get there ahead of him I might spook the elk off, and it becomes a fruitless effort. As far as techniques and tactics with a client go, there's absolutely no difference between that and my own hunting.

What time of season offers the best hunting in your area (and the highest possibility of success on trophy animals)?

Bob Fontana: September is best.
Brent Sinclair: The best is probably the rut from mid-September to the first or second week of October. That's our archery season.

How much does weather influence the hunting success in your area?

Bob Fontana: It doesn't. The only thing that can hurt you in the Rockies is lots of rain. Our hunts are relatively long—ten days. During that time you might lose one or two days to rain and

Bulls rub off the velvet wherever they find a suitable place.

fog, but it generally clears. I don't find that hot weather bothers us much in my area, because we have these little wet, seepy, timbered benches, and if it's hot that's where the bulls are going to go. We just know where to go when the weather is hot.

Brent Sinclair: Weather makes very little difference. It can be raining, windy, blowing, or whatever. You have to adapt yourself to the conditions of the day you're hunting. Cool, calm mornings without a breath of wind are probably going to give you a better opportunity, but you have to learn to adapt to hunt the area's conditions and terrain. Ours are resident elk, and so they're here all the time; we're not hunting a migratory population. We've got varied enough possibilities within our area that we can change from one setup to another if it's blowing the wrong way, and we've got that pretty well established.

How much does weather and time of season influence where and how you hunt in your area?

Bob Fontana: The more time we've spent in our area, the more we've learned to use weather patterns to determine exactly where we're going to hunt. Hot, dry conditions will put us hunting on those wet northern slopes, where there are lots of big spruce and there is heavy timber. When we get dirty weather, especially right after a storm, we'll check out the south-facing slopes and open hillsides. The weather absolutely is going to determine where we hunt.

Brent Sinclair: A little toward the end of the season, say November, our elk start coming out a bit more toward the lower end of the foothills, to get away from the snow. They start getting out on the winter range fringes late in the season. They also have to feed a lot more during the day, because it's getting colder. That makes them more visible.

Chapter 11

PACIFIC NORTHWEST GUIDES FOR ROOSEVELT ELK

Featured Guides:
Dave Fyfe, North Island Guide Outfitters, British Columbia
Bill Perkins, Wild Outdoor Adventures, Oregon

Describe your home guiding area for elk.

Dave Fyfe: Ours is classic West Coast rain forest, and the main hunting site consists of clear-cut logging areas. Vancouver Island is far more mountainous than most people think. Many people believe it's like Ireland, but it's mountainous country with high, jagged peaks. There are a lot of alpine areas, and very large regions of old-growth timber. Of course, there are many clear-cuts, all very much interspersed with a maze of logging roads. Logging and secondary roads are to us what horse trails are to guides in the north country. They are the only way we can access our hunting area.

Bill Perkins: I have hunted the Saddle Mountain area of Oregon all of my life. We hunt an area of renewed forest, old-growth forest, salmonberries, devil's cane, and blackberries. It is not all that much fun to fight the thick underbrush, but the elk are in those areas. You just have to go in after them.

What are some distinctions that set it apart?

Dave Fyfe: There is no general open hunting season for elk, because it's all on a draw system. Residents have to get a draw tag, and it's difficult to get drawn: Odds are between 80 and 120 to 1 against being drawn, which means that most people on Vancouver Island will never be drawn in their lifetime. Because of that, resident hunters tend to be inexperienced and don't know where the elk are located. For guides and outfitters there

Jim Stewart and Dave Fyfe with another terrific Vancouver Island Roosevelt bull.

is a very small quota available to nonresident hunters. Because of those two factors, we have some truly giant elk. The average ages we're taking are from ten to sixteen years.

    Bill Perkins: The Saddle Mountain area is a three-point and above zone, which is different from much of coastal Washington and Oregon. That rule gives you a decent chance at getting a good bull and not just a spike.

Why should a hunter hire a guide, as opposed to being self-guided?

Dave Fyfe: The number one thing is that without a guide, a person has no idea what the trophy quality is in an area. With our experience, we know bulls in the 300 class, and that's a pretty impressive bull. But it's not what we're after. We're able to distinguish those from bulls in the 350 class or better. With no point of reference, a guy has no idea whether he should take such a bull, or if there's a better one nearby.

Bill Perkins: Hiring a guide in an area that you have never been in will give you a better chance of being successful in a shorter period of time. If you are guiding yourself you will be spending most of your time trying to get to know the area and finding out where the elk roam. A good guide already knows that, which means you will be hunting in the right area for an elk from the very start.

What is your success rate on trophy animals?

Dave Fyfe: One hundred percent on opportunities.

Bill Perkins: I feel I have been blessed with my success. My father, who shot forty-nine bulls in his lifetime, taught me the skills I possess today. I have shot thirty Roosevelt bulls and have guided fifteen more people to a bull. All the people that I have guided have taken their first bull within three years of starting to hunt with me. Most have had chances every year, but for various reasons things didn't work out. They came back until they were successful.

Describe your usual hunting method and any common variations.

Dave Fyfe: For us here on the island, prescouting is everything. We hunt specific animals. We do a sort of inventory, always with the knowledge that we may run across a bigger bull. For the most part, though, our hunters are killing

The author poses with a giant Roosevelt bull he shot on Vancouver Island.

bulls that we've spotted before. We get on high vantage points and do a lot of spotting and endless glassing. During the rut, Roosevelt bulls tend to be in the valley bottoms. That's where the cows are during the rut, because it's easier traveling there. So getting up high and looking down on the clearings is our number one technique.

Bill Perkins: Our usual hunting method depends entirely on the season. I spend a lot of time during deer season spotting and getting to know the habits of the elk, as well as finding signs of the ones I want to hunt. If it is the early season, we drive and spot a lot. By the second season the elk are usually deep in the brush, and we go after them where they are.

How do you hunt differently with a client/hunter, as opposed to when hunting alone (for yourself)?

Dave Fyfe: I can't honestly think of anything I do differently. My son and my wife have both drawn tags twice, and we've done exactly the same for them. I still haven't drawn, so I'm speaking of family here.

Bill Perkins: I don't hunt differently! I take them on the same hunts that I go on by myself. We work the same areas in the same way. Because this technique has been working, I keep right on doing the same things that have been successful in the past.

What time of season offers the best hunting in your area (and the highest possibility of success on trophy animals)?

Dave Fyfe: We can't hunt in September, which is the peak of the rut. Our hunt starts October 10, and the second rut is on. I'm not sure it isn't actually the best time, and I'll tell you why. The animals in September commonly have fifteen to twenty-five cows with them. By October the herds are splintered, because those big bulls just don't have enough in the tank to hold the cows together. When they're in smaller herds, they're actually easier to hunt. There are a lot fewer eyes looking at you when you start to make your stalk.

Enjoying the grandeur while packing in.

Bill Perkins: I like the second season. You don't have so much road-racing going on at that time. Late in the year it seems there are a lot fewer people in the woods, even though there are the same number of tags allocated. I enjoy going after the elk in their habitat rather than running from landing to landing (logging loading areas) and glassing the clear-cuts.

How much does weather influence the hunting success in your area?

Dave Fyfe: Overall, weather is not that critical. We have a fairly moderate climate here; it's not that cold. The one thing that kills us is fog. We go to bed a little concerned about that. We're hunting specific animals in specific clear-cuts, and fog can just kill us. Getting up high and glassing down is simply impossible in the fog.

Bill Perkins: I feel that the weather plays a big part in our success.

How much does weather and time of season influence where and how you hunt in your area?

Dave Fyfe: Again, fog is the big concern. When it happens and hangs on, we move quietly into known elk areas and look for them. It becomes much more up-close and personal hunting, as opposed to long-distance spotting.

Bill Perkins: If it has been dry, it is very difficult going through the woods and trying to sneak up on an elk, so we have to modify our approach. Wind will have them holed up in certain areas, depending on its direction. Rain and snow will have them in the second-growth forest, lying down most of the time. You definitely have to change your hunting technique depending on the weather, but the way you change it depends on the situation.

Chapter 12

PARTING SHOTS BY THE ELK GUIDES

Do you have any unusual hunting stories to share?

John Caid: I was hunting with the late Prince Abdorreza, the shah of Iran's brother, and he had a .270 inlaid with gold, one of the most beautiful rifles I've ever seen—but also one of the heaviest. I carried it in a sheepskin-lined bag the entire week. We finally found a bull that the prince wanted to take, so I pulled out the rifle and handed it to him. We were forty to fifty yards from the bull, and he fired. The bull didn't even flinch. It didn't move. It didn't react. The bull was broadside but facing the other way. The prince jacked in another shell and fired again. The bull still didn't move, didn't do anything, didn't react. The prince looked over at me, and I shrugged my shoulders. I was beginning to feel guilty—as if maybe I'd bumped his rifle and knocked his scope off. He jacked a third shell in and fired a third time. This time the bull's hind leg lifted into the air, like an involuntary motion, and then came back down again—but it still didn't move. Then the bull walked off into the trees. The prince looked at me, and I didn't know what to say. At that moment we heard the bull go down—it just crashed! We hurried over, and the prince had put three bullets in a place the size of a softball, right through the lungs of this bull, and it never reacted at all. I couldn't believe it! I had been feeling terribly guilty up to that point.

I also hunted with Helmut Swarovski, owner of Swarovski Optik, one time. He was one of the nicest gentlemen I've ever hunted with. He was so interested in everything—rocks, sunsets, everything—a very pleasant man to hunt with. We were driving along toward a different hunting area when Helmut suddenly yelled, "Stop! Stop! Stop!" I thought he'd seen a big bull, so I slammed on the brakes so hard I thought we were

Elk country.

both going to have whiplash. He had my heart really pounding—until he jumped out to get a picture of the sunset.

Allen Morris: I call this my two-headed bull story. We were walking along following a herd, and there was a 6x6 bull. I put a hunter to the left twenty yards, and a hunter to the right twenty yards, and I called once. That six-point bull turned and ran straight to me. I didn't have any cover, so I had to throw myself on my back. I heard the bull run up to me to within about ten yards. He was sitting there panting, looking at me, and I said to myself, *Jay* (my hunter), *shoot him in the heart!* I knew the bull was standing there, and I knew my hunter was at full draw, but nothing happened. So I said to myself, *OK, Barry* (my other hunter), *shoot.* Of course the bull finally winded me, whirled, and took off.

I called Jay over to me and asked, "OK, Jay, what happened?"

And he said, "Well, Al, that bull was kind of head-on to me and I just didn't like the angle, so I didn't take the shot."

I waved him back to where he was, and I called Barry over and said, "Barry, what happened?"

And he said, "Well, Al, that bull was kind of head-on to me and I just didn't like the angle, so I didn't take the shot."

I shook my head and told Barry this that had to be the first two-headed bull on the ranch! Barry and Jay got into an argument over which of them the bull was head-on to.

We hadn't gone another fifty yards, and as God is my witness, I called in another 5x5 bull. We were in the midst of a million quakies. This bull walked about fifteen yards in front of Jay, who loosed an arrow; it went *thump* and stuck in a tree. The bull circled on around and ran about twenty yards and stopped right in front of Barry. He shot, and his arrow made a big thump as it struck a tree, too. And the bull ran off.

I walked over and reached down and tried to get Jay's arrow out of the tree. I said, "Well, I found your arrow, Jay, but I don't know where Barry's is."

And he said, "Look up."

In the exact same quakie was Barry's arrow, ten feet off the ground! I'm telling you, we were in a million quakies, and their arrows were stuck in the exact same quakie! If you calculated those odds, with a bull that was twenty to thirty yards away at different angles on two different archers, that they would shoot the exact same quakie on a miss—it's incredible. You couldn't make up something like that.

Jack Atcheson Jr.: The one story that comes to mind occurred when I was twelve years old. I was just starting to hunt elk and carry a rifle legally. I went out with my dad and got a beautiful five-point bull elk. I went out the second year, thirteen years old and quite naive, and hunted hard. As I kind of had suspected I might, near the end of the season I got a six-point bull elk. Now reaching the ripe age of fourteen, I really had it in the back of my mind that I had gotten a five-point the first time, then a six-point the next year, so this is the year I would get a seven-pointer. I really thought that. We went out and hunted our butts off, and we weren't seeing any elk at all. I was beating my dad up pretty bad to find me an elk, and I remember that I was sitting on a frozen elk gut pile. There were some elk feet lying there, and I jokingly told my dad I was going to rub one of them for good luck.

Five minutes later, along came a spike bull elk, which I shot and finally put down. I have that spike bull elk mounted in my office now, and it's the only bull elk I have mounted there. I call that my reminder bull. Whenever I get a little carried away in my thinking about anything, I look up at my spike bull elk and take a deep breath and remember. Elk hunting can come easy, but it can also be really tough. I just don't want to forget that lesson.

Chad Schearer: Back in the mid-1990s I was guiding for another outfitter, and we had a horrendous snowstorm. There was more than thirty inches of snow in the area, and we had about six or eight people in camp. At the start of each day we would load the horses into the trailer and haul them down into another area twenty to thirty miles from headquarters, and then ride in on BLM or Forest Service land to hunt. One morning it was nasty and snowing, the trucks are all ready, and we were heading out to hunt. On the way up the hill, one of the trucks started to slide as it neared the top. It couldn't make it all the way up the hill even though we were just a half-mile from the ranch. The horse trailer slid down into a deep ditch and got stuck.

Well, the two guys scheduled to hunt with the guide who was in trouble became belligerent and mean, shouting that this was their hunt and that they had paid good money for it, and how could he get stuck and cost them hunting time, and that sort of thing—really giving the poor guy a bad time and just going nuts.

Just then some other hunters who were hunting with us pulled in behind, and I pulled in behind them, and we all watched those two guys going nuts. Those first hunters were raising Cain, and the two hunters behind them finally said, "You know what, why don't we switch guides? We're not in that big of a rush. We've got all week. You take our guides and our trailer and horses, go on down, and go do it."

The hunters with me said, "Yeah, we'll stay here and help, too, and try to get him out of there."

So the belligerent pair took them up on the offer and left. Well, the sun came up, and we were trying to get the truck and trailer freed when all of a sudden an enormous herd of migrating elk came by, right past the truck in the ditch. All four of the hunters who had stayed to help shot bull elk right on the spot! The two that had made all that trouble didn't even see an elk that day! There is a God, and He has a sense of humor!

Van Hale: I had a guy hang himself off the saddle horn of his horse with the strap of his binocular one time. We were hunting horseback, and this hunter was a little guy, about five-one or five-two. I had him on a great, big horse, probably sixteen hands. He was a real fireball, this guy, and every time we'd see elk he was right off his horse, had his horse tied up, and was ready to shoot something immediately. He was really on the ball.

We were riding down a trail one day, and a whole herd of elk ran across in front of us. I jumped off immediately and ran over to the edge of the canyon. I reached back for him because he was always right there, and I wanted to tell him that the bull in the back was the best one. He was gone!

Then I heard all this gagging and hacking and carrying on, and there he hung, with his feet about a foot off the ground. He'd reached over to grab his rifle out of the scabbard, and when he did his binocular strap looped around the saddle horn. He'd gotten so excited that he bailed off the wrong side of the horse to get over to me more quickly, and when he did it just hung him! I'd hunted with this guy quite a few times, so I counted him a friend, but I was laughing so hard I couldn't talk. He did get an elk later in the hunt, but he didn't get that one!

Ross Johnson: I could write a whole book of stories. The one that stands out is the hunter who was taking a crap and shot a bear when he was butt-naked. We were actually hunting lions, and the hunter had his bow. A cowboy had ridden in and found a fresh lion kill, and we were hiking to check it out. We had gotten to a fork in the canyon when the hunter felt nature's call and wandered off behind a boulder.

He left his bow with me and disappeared, and then I heard something. There was a bear, standing up on his hind feet. He was a really big bear, probably a twenty-inch skull. I had a bear tag, and so did the hunter. I picked up the hunter's bow, but I couldn't even draw it because it was set on ninety pounds. I had to find that hunter. I crept around behind the rocks, and there he was, all bent over with his pants down around his ankles. I whispered, "Shoot the bear, shoot the bear!"

He was trying to wipe himself, and I was trying to get him to forget it and shoot the bear. He finally stood up, still trying to pull up his pants, and looked over a little knoll. When he saw the bear he dropped his pants, which fell down around his ankles, and let fly an arrow. That bear had heard us, though, and it came straight at us. I had a pistol, but I had left it behind when I rushed to find my hunter. The bear was trying to get to the hunter, but he was hit so hard he couldn't quite make it to him.

I went for the gun and ran back, and there was the hunter, who had made it about five feet with his pants down around his ankles. He was bent over at full draw, with the dead bear five feet away. I told him the bear was dead, but if I'd fired my gun I might have shot the hunter instead of the bear I was laughing so hard.

Another wilderness stream crossing.

Ask the Elk Guides

Ron Dube: I was guiding an elk hunter one time in November. He had a late-season permit in Sunlight Basin in extreme northwestern Wyoming. The elk there traditionally migrate out of Yellowstone Park in late November and December when we have lots of snow. I drew one of those tags myself a few years ago. We didn't have the snow, the bulls didn't come out, and I killed a cow the last day of the season.

I was guiding this client when we spotted what appeared to be a B&C elk. We made a long, circuitous stalk on horseback to get in close. A resident, however, a local person who had left camp later than we had, shot that elk from a great distance—he shot a box of shells at the animal. He ended up shooting three legs out from under the bull. He was eventually able to get close enough to finish him off, so we lost our opportunity on that great bull.

But we didn't abort the hunt. We kept working hard and went higher and higher. I'm a firm believer in hunting for sign and being able to read it. I believe that's more important than actually hunting for the animal. We got as high as we could, till the snow got too deep for the horses, and then we had to turn around and go back.

We were just running out of daylight when I spotted some tracks in our trail that had not been there when we rode up. I got off my horse and examined them, then followed them to the elk's bed. There was some discolored material in the bed that I could not identify, so I knew that there was something wrong with this elk. I knew it was a big bull from the tracks, though, so we followed it for a few hundred yards. I felt confident that we would find this elk and kill it, and we did. It was about a 340 bull.

We discovered that somebody had shot it in the mouth maybe a week before. The discolored material in the bed was from the wound. Obviously the elk would have died, because its jaw was broken. We were most glad not only that we had taken a great elk but also that we had recovered a wounded animal, instead of its being wasted. The client was pleased, and I was gratified that I had been able to identify and follow the sign.

Packing out a wilderness elk.

Rick Trusnovec: We had a Vietnam veteran hunting with us a few years ago who had been a sniper during the war. You'd think he'd be as cool as they come. We put this fellow in front of a bull, and he proceeded to think he was shooting at it. However, he only thought he was pulling the trigger. He shucked out all his shells, one at a time, without ever firing a shot. Then he turned to his guide and said he needed more bullets because the elk wasn't going down! This guy was a highly decorated soldier, but we eventually had to tell him to pick the shells up off the ground so he could reuse them!

Bob Fontana: We had a French Canadian hunter with us several years ago, a tough guy who was a veterinarian by trade. I had spotted two big bulls, so we climbed up on top of a high mountain and chased them around. We finally got one of them to come in, and he was standing there at about sixty yards on a steep hillside. The Canadian shot at the bull and knocked it tail end over teakettle, and it fell into a deep ravine.

I had a young guide with me, and he started slapping this guy on the back and congratulating him as the bull went out of sight.

I said we'd better not be shaking anybody's hand until we've got those antlers in our hands. We went to the ravine, and, of course, the bull was gone—it had completely disappeared. I looked all over and couldn't find that elk. We finally gave up and went back down the mountain.

Next morning I decided that I wanted to go back in there again, because there was another good bull there. Elk had still been bugling when we left, but I hadn't wanted to pursue them the night before, not being sure of the situation. So we went back to the exact same spot, and we bugled and bugled. About 2:00 P.M. we bugled a big bull in and shot it when it was about thirty yards away. We walked up to it and found that this elk had a bullet hole clean through its ear; the bullet had creased the base of the skull, just enough to knock it down the hill. It was the same bull we had shot the day before! It died within ten feet of where it had been shot the first time!

Brent Sinclair: I've got so many I'd like to share. One involved not an elk but a bull moose. I know now that if you've got to go in on a wounded bull moose, you darn sure don't want to do it without something to protect you. I've experienced that one before. I got a little bit hooked up that time and got thrown up in the air by a crippled bull. It was a bad deal, all the way around. I'm certain the same principle applies to a wounded bull elk. I'm lucky to be alive and in one piece after that one.

Dave Fyfe: Every story is unusual and unique, but I'll share one that illustrates the need for mental preparation. There are two brothers who have hunted with us many times; they come every other year. They came up in 2000, and both took huge B&C bulls, which were real trophies. They had rebooked for 2002, and the first brother then called. He said that he already had a great bull, and he wondered if he could ever get a better one. He told me that he was prepared to stick it out for the whole hunt and not kill an animal, in order to get a top ten B&C elk. He prepared himself mentally for not killing just any animal by holding out for something truly exceptional.

I hadn't spoken with the second brother, who had also taken a really giant elk on the previous hunt. This second brother arrived concerned that by holding out he might not get an elk at all. We ran into some resident hunters the first morning out, and this second brother panicked! Here it was opening morning, and someone was in ahead of us; he got really agitated about that. The upshot was that the second brother shot a decent Roosevelt elk that very first day, and he insisted on shooting it against our recommendations. It was not nearly as large as his earlier one, not even in the range of what we were trying to get for our hunters, and he wasn't at all happy with that bull.

Now the first brother, who had told me he was willing to go home without an elk, went eight days with bad luck at every turn. On day eight, the number four B&C bull walked out for him. And on that day we were watching three other monsters at the same time. Brother number two was there

Packing into Sky Lakes Wilderness for elk.

for all of this, unfortunately, and was he ever disappointed he had shot so early. Mental preparation is everything!

Bill Perkins: Earlier I said to let the people that are guiding you know your abilities. A couple of years ago a guy asked me to help him get a deer. He hadn't seen a deer for two weeks, but he said he wanted me to go with him and help him get one on a Saturday. He had both a doe and a buck tag. We got the doe within the first hour of daylight. Then we went off to do our best to get him a buck.

I took him on a long walking hunt where there are some good bucks in the area. I put him on a stand and told him I would circle him and try to drive some deer by him. When I came back he was gone, forcing me to look for him. I found him two hundred yards from where I had left him. That naturally made me think I'd better watch him, since he might not understand the concept of sitting still. I decided to let him do some walking to get it out of his system, and I laid out the area for him till I thought he felt comfortable. I told him to go up an old skid road about two hundred yards and sit where he could see a good distance all around him. I told him that I would return in about forty-five minutes to an hour and try to drive some deer his way. On my way back, I saw several different deer tracks going in his direction.

I wasn't quite back to him when I heard a shot from his direction, so I thought he had gotten one. When I got to where he should have been, however, he was nowhere to be found, so I whistled and then yelled. Finally, I thought maybe he had gone back to the truck, thinking I would meet him there. To my dismay, there was nobody at the truck. So I drove up and down the road that paralleled the drive we were on, and finally I heard twelve pistol shots. I blew the horn, and he came out of the woods looking a little sheepish.

I asked, "How big a deer did you get?"

"None," he said. "I was lost and fired those last shots to summon help."

Now what makes this interesting is that this man teaches survival techniques for the sheriff's department here in Oregon. Yet he couldn't explain why he had fired the shot at a deer and

Horses allow hunters to cover large areas on wilderness elk hunts.

then disobeyed my instructions to stay put. We still had two hours of daylight left, and I didn't let him out of the truck again. We drove the roads the last two hours so I wouldn't have to spend all night looking for him.

What do you see as the most critical environmental/management/ public relations issues affecting the future of hunting elk?

John Caid: I think the most critical thing for all hunting is getting the kids involved. I have three daughters who hunt, and it's critical that every hunter get kids into hunting. In Arizona, it's tough to keep the kids involved because they can't get drawn for tags. My daughters drew a couple of times for turkeys— and they love hunting turkeys—but we couldn't get drawn for three to four years for deer, turkey, or anything. Keeping kids involved is critical to keeping elk hunting, deer hunting, in fact all hunting going. I think my fondest memories of the best hunts I've ever been on have been with my daughters, mainly spring turkey hunting. To be able to go every year with kids would do a lot to save hunting for everybody.

Ask the Elk Guides

Allen Morris: Public relations are number one. Through the RMEF and other conservation organizations and funds, we're trying to save as much elk environment, especially winter range, as possible. The state agencies are doing the best they can with management. The battle we're losing as hunters is with public relations. We need to portray hunting as positive, that hunters are good people, and that hunters are the reason there are more elk than there have ever been.

We're putting dollars on the ground for the animals instead of sending it to some animal-rights organization where the head man is driving around in a limousine and has an executive suite in New York City. The money we're putting on the ground is going to the animals. People say, "Well, you just want to protect them to kill them." No, we want to protect these animals because we truly love them. We're hunters. It's in our blood. We've been hunting for thousands of years, and it's how humanity has subsisted. We need to portray hunters as good people who raise good families. You give me a cross-section of the United States, and I'll take the hunters over the guys who eat tofu and watch the Golf Channel. I think they're better people who raise better kids.

We're losing the public relations battle, though, because there are generations of people who think that beef is the cellophane-wrapped hamburger they buy at the grocery store. They don't understand that an animal died to produce that. Killing an animal is a part of hunting, but we need to show them that it's also rendering that animal for its meat. It's feeding our families. We've got to do a better job of portraying hunters in a good light.

Jack Atcheson Jr.: We've got a good elk population right now, but we've got a thought process developing, at least in Montana, that there are too many elk. That's a critical problem. We don't have too many elk. We're just starting to see enough elk. There are 150,000 elk here, and you can go out and see herds of elk fairly often. But it's kind of a gridlock between some landowners and cattle interests and those who want vibrant herds of wild game. A lot of people want limits put on elk populations, and the elk in this state live a lot on public lands. Some people want to reserve those blades of grass for nothing but beef animals, so they want Montana Fish and Game to start reducing elk populations. As a sportsman, I don't want to see them reduced—I want to see them increased. The sad part about it is that the habitat here could support an increase.

Predator management is also a huge thing. Wolves are one piece in the predator puzzle. You've heard about the wolves nailing all the elk down around Yellowstone Park. Everyone's talking about that, but that's just a part of the problem. There are also lots of grizzlies and black bears. They tagged fifty elk cows last spring in the northern part of Yellowstone, and 60 percent of those elk cows were dead within a month, all of them killed by grizzlies and black bears. The wolves are going to get the rest of them by year's end. The wolf was just that missing piece, with bears getting 60 percent, but the 40 percent went on and were able to maintain or even increase the herd in some areas. Now the wolves have stepped in, and the package is complete. The predator issue is super big.

Between predators and the erroneous perception that we have too many elk, we've got a real problem. The Forest Service will come up and say, well, we've got this elk management area here in Montana or Idaho, and we want you guys to put a limit on how many elk there are in it. That really bothers me, because we've got lots of food here. We need to protect winter range, where wolves are now chasing the elk off. There are a lot of things that are putting elk hunting in danger.

Chad Schearer: One of the biggest issues is predators and predator control. We're seeing a tremendous downturn of elk numbers down in the Yellowstone area because of wolf predation. There are some great things going on with the RMEF as far as increasing and protecting elk habitat. Unfortunately, I'm seeing a lot of things going on with predators that are unsettling, including black and grizzly bears. I truly believe it's part of an animal-rights ploy to decrease game populations and deprive hunters of their prey. It will have the biggest impact on the younger generation, because if you hike with a twelve-year-old for twenty miles and he doesn't see an animal, it's hard to hold his enthusiasm for hunting.

Van Hale: Game management is going to be our biggest challenge, keeping everybody from Game and Fish to the Forest Service to the general public on the same page. The nonhunting public needs to be educated as to why we still need to hunt and harvest game, because we're so far outnumbered that we need their support when things come to a vote. Hunters need to be acutely aware of the need to work together with government agencies and the general public to ensure the future of hunting.

Ross Johnson: Vehicles off the road and trash accumulating in the back country are critical issues to elk hunting. Every year

Brent and son Tanner Sinclair with Tanner's first bull.

people create new roads where none existed before. Eventually, that's going to start shutting down the good hunting.

Ron Dube: Prior to 1988 and the Yellowstone fires, outfitter success in northwest Wyoming averaged around 50 percent. If a guy had twenty hunters, he killed ten elk. If he had forty hunters, he killed twenty elk. After the fires of 1988, however, when a lot of that canopy burned away, you could see elk in what formerly was green timber. What used to be their bedding cover was now open, but they were still using it. Since you could see them, you could shoot from one ridge to another. Success rates shot up after 1988 from 50 percent to 80 or 90 percent. For a period of several years the rates stayed high. By 1994, I thought we were killing too many elk. But in 1995 success was even better! Things aren't as good now as in 1995, which was a banner year, but things are holding steady. I believe that's because northwest Wyoming is an elk factory.

However, I do believe that we're going to see a decline in success rates because of the large numbers of wolves that we now have. These were introduced in 1995, and unfortunately they're eating a lot of calves.

On another issue, we need to improve the image of hunters as sportsmen and ethical people. People in general need to learn that hunting is a part of our genetic makeup. It's not a sport. The majority of people may view hunting as recreation and sport, but we've been hunting ever since the days of the cave men. If more people could come to understand the sacred, natural relationship between the hunter and wildlife, then everybody would benefit. Everything that we all do to follow the guidelines of ethical, responsible behavior goes a long way toward achieving our goal of passing on the tradition and heritage of hunting to future generations.

Rick Trusnovec: Wolves are the big issue for elk hunters. We've got them in our area, and we've had them since they dumped them here in 1995. It is affecting how we hunt. Probably the most difficult thing is finding that places which always had game now have no elk. Wolves haven't destroyed us, but they sure do bump the elk off some of our ridges and can make them hard to find.

Bob Fontana: Enclosure-type hunting, where a guy goes into a small, fenced-in area and shoots something with big numbers, is leaving us exposed to antihunting sentiment. Because of where we hunt, access management is also important to us. I think logging and some other activities on the land base are good for elk habitat, but you've got to manage that access very stringently. Logging is good for elk, but we need to be aware what that increased opportunity can do to elk populations. And that's not just during hunting season, but at all times of the year. The proliferation of ATVs is a related problem that really sticks in my craw.

Brent Sinclair: Habitat loss and increased numbers of predators are the big issues. These elk are adaptable, but we need to understand that they've got certain minimal requirements. In some areas predators are really a factor in elk populations, especially the calves.

Dave Fyfe: Education of the nonhunting public is important to the future of elk hunting. Here on Vancouver Island, a lot of residents don't even know there are elk on the island, so their knee-jerk reaction when a hunting question comes up is, *Should we be hunting those things?* It happens! It's been a weakness of the hunting community all along. SCI has been a leader in education, along with the RMEF, and I salute them for their efforts. But as hunters we haven't done a good job of educating people who don't hunt about hunting. A little education makes the lights come on for most people.

Bill Perkins: In Oregon the most critical thing I see is that our seasons and the animals we hunt are tied too closely to the sale of tags. The Oregon Department of Fish and Game is run by tag revenue, and they make crucial decisions based on selling more tags, not necessarily on biological reality. For instance, ours is a three-point unit with an average of twenty-three bulls per hundred cows. This is one of the highest in Oregon, but they are considering changing it back to spike-only during the early season, and then any bull during the second season. That would generate more tag revenue, to be sure, but why change something that is successful and working? They say they have done this in the Snake River Canyon, and it has worked. But they are nowhere close to our bull-to-cow ratio there. Additionally, the Snake River area has a different type of elk and completely different habitat and terrain.

Do you have any parting words of wisdom for elk hunters?

John Caid: In order to settle on an outfitter, hunters need to talk to more than just the outfitter or guide. They need to get those references and talk to everybody they can about the hunting area, about the quality of the bulls, and the like. It's really important that they do their homework before they book a hunt, because there are a lot of new outfitters out there, and like all small businesses, 90 percent fail the first year. Since that's the case, they just can't give you your money's worth. I know most hunters work as hard for their money as I do for mine, and they'd best make sure they get their money's worth.

Allen Morris: Wayne Carlton taught me how to call elk twenty years ago, but the best thing he ever told me was, "You need to go find some elk and spend some time with them." Well, here I am twenty years later, running one of the best ranches in the country. The reason I did it is that I went out and got close to the elk and let the elk teach me. Guys can read this book and glean a lot of knowledge from it, but if they don't physically get off the couch and quit watching the Outdoor Channel and get out into the wild and listen to elk bugle in September, reading a book won't do them a bit of good.

Jack Atcheson Jr.: If you haven't tried it, get out and do it. It's the greatest hunting there is. I've hunted sheep all my life, but there's nothing quite like elk hunting. You can get a license relatively easily, you don't have to draw a tag, and when it comes to taking a decent elk, there are lots of them. It's never been better than it is right now. Getting a bigger bull might be a little tougher than it was at one time, depending on where you go, but don't wait. Go now, because in ten years it could be a whole different story.

Chad Schearer: There have been a lot of elk taken at the eleventh hour. Don't give up until the very last day. So often a guy will hunt it hard and finally say, "You know, it's not going to happen." What I tell people is that you can't kill a bull elk by sitting in camp. You've got to be out there hunting, even when chances seem low. Elk are harvested out in the field.

Van Hale: Stay in shape and shoot straight.

Ross Johnson: Think positive, don't quit, don't give up. I've seen guys hunt just two days, then if they haven't seen a bull they leave. I've seen more elk killed in the last hour of the last day than I have the first hour of the first day. The main thing is to keep on hunting. If there's some kind of problem with your outfitter or guide, finish the hunt before confronting it.

Ron Dube: Don't give up, and take the endeavor seriously if you want to be successful. Practice and become as proficient as possible at all aspects of outdoorsmanship.

Rick Trusnovec: Don't get so hung up on the Outdoor Channel, or on videos in which you see all those big bulls being called in or harvested. Too many hunters come out with false expectations that elk hunting is pretty easy. You've got to have the right mentality to enjoy hunting elk. The first thing is that you've got to enjoy being out in a wilderness area. Hunt as hard as you can. Don't expect to see elk as often as you see whitetails in your home hunting area. Don't let what you see on television or video inflate your expectations of what an elk hunt is like, because you can be misled. It can even ruin your hunt.

Bob Fontana: I don't know if it's wisdom, but get out and do it. Do it while you're still able to do it. Do it to enjoy it, and make it a habit, as opposed to just going out to collect an elk. I think elk are one of those fascinating species, like white-tailed deer, that you should hunt every year. Don't look at elk hunting as an acquisition type of hunt, the way you would a mountain goat hunt, where the terrain is tough, the hunt is physically demanding, and you really don't want to do it too often. Elk hunting is a kind of hunting in which you want to develop a relationship with the area you hunt and with your guide. And you'll enjoy it a lot more if you come back several times. Elk hunters used to do it more that way, whether they did it all themselves or hired an outfitter. That used to be the norm.

Brent Sinclair: Hunt hard: Life's short.

Dave Fyfe: Be proactive in issues related to antihunters and educating the public. When you do go hunting, be mentally prepared. If you have to kill an elk to have a successful hunt, you're setting yourself up for disappointment.

Bill Perkins: Have patience and do your homework on the area you are going to hunt. Then know your ability and the ability of your equipment. Remember to enjoy the outdoors and our right to be there. Someday that might be gone if we don't keep fighting for our right to hunt and to bear arms.

Tribute

Robert Bruce Fontana, owner/operator of Elk Valley Bighorn Outfitters, died in a tragic hunting accident in Tanzania on Saturday, July 17, 2004. He was hunting with Paddy Curtis of Luke Samaras Safaris. Bob and Paddy were hunting lesser kudu in very thick brush when a buffalo charged the two men from the side. Paddy Curtis fired and hit the buffalo; however, by the time he fired, the buffalo had already reached Fontana. The buffalo gored Bob, leaving him mortally wounded. The pair had not been hunting buffalo, and there was no indication that the buffalo had been previously wounded before it attacked. Bob Fontana was forty-seven years old.

Bob was a very successful outfitter, guiding hunters in the magnificent mountain landscape of the upper Elk River valley in British Columbia. This area supports a diverse and abundant wildlife population, and, combined with Bob's strong marketing skills, his passion for hunting, and his dynamic personality, he had clients from all over the world, many on a repeat basis. He was the consummate professional: attentive to every detail of his work, a dedicated supporter of the industry, tremendously knowledgeable about wildlife and wildlife issues, and absolutely committed to wildlife conservation and management. He was also a partner with the Lancaster family of Nahanni Butte Outfitters.

Bob leaves behind Anna, his wife of eleven years; their two children, Kaitlin and Callie; and a twin sister, Barbara Endicott. A fitting epitaph to Bob's life is a statement he, himself, once made: Every man dies . . . not every man lives. He will be sorely missed.

NOTES

NOTES

NOTES

NOTES

NOTES

NOTES

NOTES

NOTES